1969

This book may be kept

FOURTEEN DAYS

BYRON AND THE DYNAMICS OF METAPHOR

BYRON AND THE DYNAMICS OF METAPHOR

W. Paul Elledge

VANDERBILT UNIVERSITY PRESS *Nashville*

for *Mother and Dad*

Acknowledgments

Two consecutive summer grants from the Vanderbilt University Research Council materially assisted the completion of this manuscript. The editors of *Keats-Shelley Journal* have graciously consented to the expansion here of an essay which originally appeared in their publication; and the editors of *Journal of English and Germanic Philology, Studies in English Literature,* and *Tennessee Studies in Literature* have permitted me to withdraw articles from their journals when projected dates of publication coincided with the appearance of this book.

Several friends and associates deserve special citation. Professor Edgar Hill Duncan of the Vanderbilt University English Department read the entire manuscript and offered several valuable suggestions. Miss Mary Lee Tipton and Mrs. Walter H. Deathridge executed their editorial and secretarial responsibilities with uncompromising thoroughness and good humor. To Professor William H. Marshall's studies of Byron, I obviously owe a good deal, but, beyond that, his sensitive and meticulous criticism of my manuscript alerted me to numerous indiscretions and oversights. Finally, my continuing personal and professional debt to Professor Richard Harter Fogle can only in part be discharged by formal acknowledgment; to his counsel, patience, generosity, and wisdom belongs much of the credit for whatever may be worthwhile in these pages.

W. P. E.

Nashville, Tennessee

vii

Contents

Commotion Is the Extremest Point

Zwei Seelen Wohnen, ach! in meiner Brust!

—Goethe

WHEN, in August 1966, one of the essays now incorporated into this study was returned to me by a major American journal, the editor justified his rejection by reminding me of Lord Byron's professed scorn for poetic craftsmanship and of scholarly precedent which considered the poetry a melodramatized diary brimful of the author's loneliness, despair, guilt, and eloquent theatricality. To my essay I added one paragraph insisting upon the desirability of examining the art of Byron's poetry, mailed the piece to another journal, and received this criticism with the acceptance letter in April 1967: "It is now a cliché to begin an essay on Byron by saying that we must turn from irrelevancies like biography to the poetry itself. Elledge should steer clear of this particular cliché."

The incident is unfortunately symptomatic of the antithetical critical attitudes toward Byron's artistic seriousness and skill; and despite the efforts of Knight, Marshall, Marchand, and Joseph,[1] among others,[2] it dramatizes the need still incumbent upon the Byron

1. G. Wilson Knight, "The Two Eternities: An Essay on Byron," in *The Burning Oracle* (New York: Oxford University Press, 1939); William H. Marshall, *The Structure of Byron's Major Poems* (Philadelphia: University of Pennsylvania Press, 1962); M. K. Joseph, *Byron the Poet* (London: V. Gollancz, 1964); Leslie A. Marchand, *Byron's Poetry: A Critical Introduction* (Boston: Houghton Mifflin, 1965). I regret that Robert F. Gleckner's *Byron and the Ruins of Paradise* (Baltimore: Johns Hopkins University Press, 1967) did not reach me before this book was completed.

2. Particularly: Harold Bloom, *The Visionary Company* (New York: Doubleday and Company, 1961); Samuel C. Chew, *The Dramas of Lord Byron* (New York: Russell & Russell, 1964 [reissued]); Ernest J. Lovell, Jr., *Byron: The Record of a Quest* (Austin: University of Texas Press, 1949); Karl

3

commentator briefly to vindicate himself for undertaking a primarily aesthetic investigation of the poetry. No doubt Byron's ideological and emotional instability, his hatred of systems and system-spinners, and his wearisome sneers at his own conscious artistry seem *ipso facto* to sabotage any search for aesthetic consistency or homogeneity, or, often, even thematic coherence. No doubt Byron wished his contemporaries to believe he took his art no more seriously than he took his charades and his women. But the evidence of his texts, once located and unprejudicially evaluated, gives the lie to Byron's dazzling deceptive tactics. Biographical fact and common sense must of course moderate exercises in critical ingenuity—particularly in Byron's case—but the pioneer work of scholars within the last twenty years has clearly alerted us to the urgency of reappraising the art of Byron's poetry. An intensive and impartial reading of representative "romantic" poems can prove that Byron possessed the artistic proficiency and integrity of which we have so long sought to deprive him.

To begin an essay on Byron by pointing to the poet's dualistic nature is perhaps a critical commonplace, but it is nevertheless the proper point of departure for any study of his poetry, not necessarily because the personality of the poet lurks threateningly beneath the verse, but because the distinguishing feature of his thought and art is a vacillation between the poles of orthodox dualism and romantic monism. All of the other paradoxes in his works are ultimately traceable to this fundamental and conscious dichotomy: the fluctuation between emphasis on intellect and emotion, classicism and relativistic subjectivism, pantheism and realism, flesh and spirit, stasis and change, spontaneity and ratiocination, impressionism and formalism, vastness and finitude, energy and ennui—this oscillation is rooted in an exceedingly flexible temperament which refused to settle on one metaphysical doctrine as the governing principle of the universe.

Kroeber, *Romantic Narrative Art* (Madison: University of Wisconsin Press, 1960); George M. Ridenour, *The Style of "Don Juan"* (New Haven: Yale University Press, 1960); Andrew Rutherford, *Byron: A Critical Study* (Stanford: Stanford University Press, 1961); and Paul West, *Byron and the Spoiler's Art* (New York: St. Martin's Press, 1961).

Byron's vision is too expansive, too encompassing, to impose upon itself a rigid and ill-fitting system of thought.

Little stock need be taken, therefore, in complaints against his insincerity, inconsistency, or lack of conscious intention. He was aware of his "failing:" "If I am sincere with myself," he admitted, "(but I fear one lies more to one's self than to anyone else), every page should confute, refute, and utterly abjure its predecessor."[3] What must be stressed, however, is Byron's absolute fidelity to accurate factual and emotional representation in his poetry, his unqualified sincerity in presenting what at any given moment his mood might have convinced him was truth. To his journal he confides: "for the soul of me, I cannot and will not give the lie to my own thoughts and doubts, come what may. If I am a fool, it is, at least, a doubting one; and I envy no one the certainty of his self-approved wisdom."[4] His chameleonic characteristics, Byron says, are "owing to the extreme *mobilité* of his nature, which yields to present impressions;"[5] and later, in the now famous passage, he defines *mobilité* as an "excessive susceptibility of immediate impressions—at the same time without *losing* the past: and is, though sometimes apparently useful to the possessor, a most painful and unhappy attribute."[6] Just so with the Coleridgian imagination, as Harold Bloom notes:

This is Byron's social version of the Romantic term "Imagination," for mobility also reveals itself "in the balance or reconciliation of opposite or discordant qualities: of sameness, with difference; the individual, with the representative; the sense of novelty and freshness, with old and familiar objects." The great Romantic contraries—emotion and order, judgment and enthusiasm, steady self-possession and profound or vehement feeling—all find their social balance in the quality of mobility.[7]

Justifiably skeptical of the stasis inherent in formalized attitudes,

3. *The Letters and Journals of Lord Byron*, edited by Rowland E. Prothero, 6 vols. (London: John Murray, Ltd., 1898–1904), II, 366, hereafter cited as *L & J.*
4. *L & J*, II, 351.
5. *Conversations of Lord Byron with the Countess of Blessington* (London: R. Bentley, 1834), p. 110.
6. Note to *Don Juan*, XVI, xcvii, 820.
7. Pp. 264–265.

Byron would interpret the denial or suppression of emotional responsiveness in deference to a conceptualized philosophy as thoroughly self-defeating. The adjective "excessive" in his definition, however, is probably apologetic, for Byron understands that sole reliance upon unpredictable affective responses may lead to intellectual chaos in a work of art. But so strong is the influence of instinctual impulse on him that he remains content to risk philosophical inconsistency in favor of a sincere representation of momentary truth.

On the matter of conscious intention, let Marshall's common sense suffice:

> It seems reasonable . . . to propose . . . that intention yields the subject, the general form, and the meaning of the poem; but organic creation, an activity that takes place primarily in the subconscious, begins where conscious and mechanical intention ceases. No work of literature was ever written that was not first constructed upon the writer's fixed and regulating intention toward that work; but no significant literary work ever failed to rise above this base, to become for the writer himself "something rich and strange" in the very process of creation. In terms of this, the critic's function is primarily to give some conscious explanation of what goes on in the work itself (presumably, then, reflecting what has gone on in the mind of the writer) at a somewhat less than conscious level.[8]

One might also note here two of many frequently overlooked comments by Byron on the revision of poetry: "Second thoughts in every thing are best, but, in rhyme, third and fourth don't come amiss."[9] And again: "in composition I do not think *second* thoughts are best, though *second* expressions may improve the first ideas."[10] The patent contradiction does not negate the patent interest in revision. Byron was no Flaubert; but as T. Guy Steffan and Willis Pratt have so ably demonstrated,[11] he retouched his manuscripts more often than he would ever publicly admit.

Morse Peckham, observing such contradictions and paradoxes in

8. P. 20.
9. *L & J*, II, 150.
10. *Ibid.*, 305.
11. *Byron's Don Juan: A Variorum Edition,* 4 vols. (Austin: University of Texas Press, 1957).

the man and the poet, once described Byron as the arch representative of "negative Romanticism;" his poetry contains "the expression of the attitudes, the feelings, and the ideas of a man who has left static mechanism but has not arrived at a reintegration of his thought and art in terms of dynamic organicism."[12] This is but another way of saying that Byron's flexibility of thought was the most characteristic feature of his mind. In all likelihood, Byron had no more abandoned a mechanistic view than he had finally accepted a dynamic view, no matter how attractive either one might have appeared. Consequently, the dialectical tension generated by his emotional desire for absolutism and his intellectual recognition of the relativistic or pluralistic had two effects: it produced in the life a psychological restiveness which eliminated any prospect of emotional stability; but it issued in poetry vital with the persistence of a questing intelligence, dubious but not despairing of terminal reconciliation.

Given the elastic and exploratory qualities of Byron's thought, then, one might expect the most frequent and representative images in his poetry to bear upon the dichotomies in man's character. To such images I wish to direct my attention, but definitions are first in order. The terms "image" (and its derivatives), "figure," "metaphor," and "configuration" are almost always used interchangeably and in their broadest senses in this study to suggest the general principle of comparison in Byron's poetry: that is, similarities, analogies, correspondences among two or more ostensibly disparate objects, concepts, or experiences are distinguished by the poet for the purpose of illuminating afresh some facet of human existence. Since poetry—even Byron's poetry, I would insist—is a severely concentrative form, the writer will necessarily not only depend to a large degree upon the evocative value—the connotative richness—of his images for the communication of his themes, but he will also require of those images clear elucidation of the complex relationships which they attempt to establish. If such relationships are made explicit, relevant, and intelligible—if, that is, some sort of order and control is imposed upon metaphorical complexity and diversity—and if the connotative value of the image assists in clarifying the idea being

---

12. "Toward a Theory of Romanticism," *PMLA*, LXVI (1951), 15.

communicated, the image may be judged successful. Byron's images, I think, function actively as complements and reinforcements to his themes; thus they represent, in small, the ultimate union of his intellectual and imaginative faculties.

"Fire" and "clay" are Byron's favorite metaphorical vehicles for illustrating the paradoxical composition of human nature: the first representing variously passion, aspiration, freedom, motion, emotion, energy, infinity, and divinity; and the second typifying intellect, frustration, bondage, ennui, sterility, finitude, and mortality. In almost every major poem, the one figure will appear with its diametric opposite either explicit or implied, as in the oft-quoted passage from *Childe Harold's Pilgrimage,* Canto III: "there is a fire / And motion of the soul which will not dwell / In its own narrow being" but would aspire to spurn "the clay-cold bonds which round our being cling." This fire-clay antinomy, however, is but one member (although the most significant one) of Byron's quartet of preferred imagistic motifs. Subordinate to it but frequently used in conjunction with it are, on the one hand, antipodal images of light and darkness, and on the other, images of organic growth and mechanical stasis— the figures of light and growth generally corresponding in symbolic and connotative value to the qualities of fire imagery noted above, and the figures of darkness and stasis having a similar relationship to clay imagery. Finally, the image of the counterpart (or the *Doppelgänger* motif) appears with sufficient frequency to merit inclusion here: the counterpart configuration may be defined as an actual or imaginary persona or phenomenon which reflects all or part of a protagonist's character, or, more precisely, what the protagonist should have been or desires to become. In each of these image patterns, polarities are juxtaposed; and, as I intend to demonstrate, the thematic purpose of the juxtaposition is twofold. Byron means first of all to figure forth the essential dichotomy of human nature, and second, to dramatize the pathos and tragedy of mortality, precipitated by man's efforts to reconcile the antithetical impulses of his being. That such a reconciliation is finally impossible is suggested again and again by Byron's antipodal imagistic construct.

The poet's assumptions about the character of human existence are not confined, of course, to metaphorical representation in these four motifs. Concomitant with them are minor figurative patterns which extend and reinforce the philosophical statements advanced through the principal imagistic substructure. The theme of man's "fatality," for instance, is frequently encapsulated in figures of decomposition and waste; or, conversely, Byron finds in the more spectacular natural phenomena—sun, moon, star, thundercloud, lightning, mountain-peak—figures to complement his representation of man's divine qualities. Tornadic winds, avalanches, inundations, and sea-tempests provide rich and evocative kinesthetic images correlative with the electrifying emotions and titanic gestures of his characters. Lower animals, insects, and reptiles, on the other hand, are often employed to reflect the baser features of man's character—his bestiality, his self-laceration, his venomous hypocrisy. These auxiliary patterns, in any case, like the four primary motifs and others to be noted later, evolve from and illustrate Byron's undergirding postulate on the contradictory inclinations of human nature.

For purposes of conciseness, clarity, and thoroughness within certain boundaries, I have somewhat arbitrarily distinguished Byron's poetic career into three periods and have selected representative, primarily nonsatiric works from each period to demonstrate the degree of his success in using thematic imagery. Before explaining my method and procedure, however, I hasten to add that my exclusion of Byron's satiric poems from this study is certainly not meant to suggest that he occupies any station lower than that of a first-rank satirist. One of the oldest and most rankling clichés of Byron criticism insists upon the division of his work into "romantic" and "classic" categories, even while one of the most easily documented characteristics of the Byron canon is the coexistence (however strained) of both elements in such pieces as *Don Juan* and *Childe Harold's Pilgrimage*. It is perhaps unjust to detach and trace the development of his poetry of sensibility from the simultaneous evolution of his ironic powers, particularly since these two opposing tendencies in Byron's constitution correspond to the view of human nature I have described as the spine of his art. Without drawing an inflexible line of distinction between types of Byronic poetry, therefore, and because George M. Ridenour and M. K. Joseph have written with some skill on the maturation of Byron's ironic or satiric style, I have found it expedient to limit this investigation to primarily nonsatiric works. My hope is that examination of poems wherein the conflicts, the characterizations, the themes, and the emphases are similar, if not identical, may enable me to trace Byron's developing competence in the use of images more thoroughly than the inclusion of chiefly satiric poems would permit.

In three of the early (1813–1815) oriental romances, *The Corsair, Lara,* and *Parisina,* Byron dramatizes the efforts of three protagonists to harmonize their visions of an ideal realm with their rational perceptions of the real world; and he reinforces these conflicts with imagistic patterns opposing sunlight and darkness, heat and cold, solidity and fragility, dreams and realities. Whatever psychological equilibrium Conrad the Corsair and Lara achieve, furthermore, is in part due to the influence of their respective counterparts, Medora and Kaled; and the depicture of Azo's *(Parisina)* attempt to integrate his intellectual faculties (presented in statuesque and metallic figures) with his emotional tendencies (presented in images of fire, sunlight, and fertile vegetation) is a clear presentiment of similar metaphorical use in Byron's later dramas.

The poems of Byron's second period (1816–1817)—*The Prisoner of Chillon, Childe Harold's Pilgrimage,* Canto III, and *Manfred*—are basically organized by the theme of the disparity between the sensuous and imaginative worlds. The inability of the Prisoner, for example, to reconcile his sensory and intellectual faculties is imaged throughout the poem in the juxtaposition of light, plant, and bird configurations with figures of darkness, stones, and chains. Harold and Manfred, both unable to bridge the gulf between the claims of the flesh and the aspirations of the spirit, attempt empathic identification with arresting natural and preternatural phenomena. Accompanying and complementing their egoistic projections are figures of meteoric flight and spectacular collapse, flaming desire and icy frustration, cosmic freedom and enslaved mortality—all of them designed to picture a mortal wracked by the incompatibility of body and soul. Additionally, the fire-clay paradox makes its first notable appearance in the Third Canto of *Childe Harold's Pilgrimage,* and the counterpart figure (Astarte) is superbly employed for thematic purposes in *Manfred.*

Three dramas, *Marino Faliero, Sardanapalus,* and *Cain,* constitute my examination of Byron's third period (1820–1821). In the first, the ethical ambivalence of the hero's thought and action—his reluctance to commit himself either to the dictates of his mind or the desires of his heart—is effectively figured in patterns of half-light; and this basic pattern is supported by minor motifs emphasizing blood, bestial, statuesque, and organic figures. In *Sardanapalus,* the twin tendencies of the hero's character toward rational and authoritative rulership and toward passivity and self-indulgence are depicted in his bisexuality; again, duality of character is marked by the opposition of metallic (or stone) figures with floral images. The evolution of Sardanapalus' "divinity," moreover, initiated and sustained by his counterpart Myrrah, is figured in images of light and darkness. Physical, intellectual, and theological darkness and light, vastness and finitude, freedom and slavery, clear-sightedness and myopia are the chief resources for Byron's imagistic explorations in *Cain:* the hero soars only to plunge, sees only to be blinded, is emancipated only to be rebound. Here, too, the figure of the counterpart finds its most singular representation in Adah, the wife and sister of the hero. Cain is indeed the most genuinely pitiable victim in Byron's works, for to him alone is verified what all the other protagonists only sense—the deplorable minuteness of man amidst the universal immensity.

The limitations of this study will be immediately apparent; they are intentional. I have included biographical matter only where it is essential to clarification; I have not sought by any systematic comparative method to fit Byron into the Romantic tradition; I am not here concerned with influences, sources, or analogues; only rarely do I relate the poems discussed in these pages to others in the canon. Consideration of such worthy issues no doubt would have enriched this study; but to undertake so many problems, as other critics may testify, is to risk diversion from and misrepresentation of the primary intention. With Byron the peril is particularly great. Because, therefore, the question of Byron as skilled craftsman is so enormously complex and controversial, I have tried to preserve a relatively circumscribed and singular focus, hoping that microscopic examination will in part compensate for telescopic loss.

My purpose is not to demonstrate any marked progression of

thought in Byron's verse or to show that the dichotomies of the poetry are finally reconciled. Byron's development must be measured in terms of multi-leveled accumulation rather than linear progression; and, judged by this standard, the rich and complex poetry of the later dramas shows a decisive advance over the crude use of imagery in the early tales. Close study of representative poetry will show that Byron recognized the value of employing imagery for thematic purposes and that he attempted to refine, to sharpen his images, to give them depth and force by accretion and particularity, and to integrate them organically with his themes. Beginning with an assumption about the duality of human character, he designed a dialectical figurative pattern to encompass the implications of his assumption, and elaborated, with impressive diversity, upon that fundamental pattern. The complexity and variety of his imagery emphatically show that

> From the star
> To the winding worm, all life is motion; and
> In life *commotion* is the extremest point
> Of life.[13]

Despite the mixture of metaphors here, the passage illustrates the poet's refusal to be restrained by any single world, philosophy, attitude, or mode of conduct. Forever spinning between the poles of dualism and monism, intellect and emotion, flesh and spirit, clay and fire, he represents with extraordinary passion and insight, through his imagery, the irreconcilable opposites which are responsible for the "commotion" of mortal existence.

13. *The Deformed Transformed,* I, ii, 590–593.

The Convulsive Dream

We look before and after,
And pine for what is not.

—Shelley

I N his oriental tales of late 1813 and after, Lord Byron was clearly exploiting a formula of narrative and character[1] that had proved immensely popular in *The Giaour* (May 1813) and *The Bride of Abydos* (November 1813); the same formula, just slightly varied, had earlier accounted for the commercial success of Cantos I and II of *Childe Harold's Pilgrimage* (March 1812) and had catapulted Byron to the apogee of the London literary scene. Principally responsible for the contemporary popularity of these tales was, of course, the same device which has since then practically blinded us to any other feature of the works: the extended delineations of that gloomy, megalomaniacal, guilt-ridden outcast now labeled "the Byronic hero."[2] This protagonist indeed looms large and imposingly in the early narratives, but we need not persist in thinking that Byron's interest centered singly on the flamboyant depicture of himself as he wished others to view him. The presence of self-dramatization does not necessarily mean that "Byron in these years did not take his poetry very seriously."[3] William H. Marshall,[4] Bernard Blackstone,[5] and M. K. Joseph[6] are the only critics to my knowl-

1. Andrew Rutherford, *Byron: A Critical Study* (Stanford: Stanford University Press, 1961), p. 38.

2. By far the best study of this "hero" is Peter Thorslev's *The Byronic Hero: Types and Prototypes* (Minneapolis: University of Minnesota Press, 1962).

3. Rutherford, p. 47.

4. *The Structure of Byron's Major Poems* (Philadelphia: University of Pennsylvania Press, 1962).

5. *The Lost Travellers* (London: Longmans, 1962), chapter vii and *passim*.

6. *Byron the Poet* (London: V. Gollancz, 1964).

edge[7] who have looked far beyond the awesome hero for a strictly aesthetic value in these narratives, but their emphases and mine are almost always different.

Familiar though they may be, certain of Byron's scattered references to the conditions under which these poems were composed and to his attitudes toward the pieces form a necessary prolegomenon to consideration of the texts. Of *The Giaour* he wrote to Gifford, "It was written . . . in a state of mind, from circumstances which occasionally occur to 'us youth,' that rendered it necessary for me to apply my mind to something, any thing but reality."[8] About *The Bride of Abydos* he commented in a letter to Moore, "All convulsions end with me in rhyme; and to solace my midnights, I have scribbled another Turkish story. . . . I have written this . . . for the sake of *employment*,—to wring my thoughts from reality, and take refuge in 'imaginings,' however 'horrible'."[9] And of *The Corsair* he remarked, "It was written in four nights to distract my dreams from————. . . . had I not done something at that time, I must have gone mad, by eating my own heart."[10] The attitude had not changed by 1815: "an addiction to poetry is very generally the result of an 'uneasy mind in an uneasy body'."[11] Byron writes, therefore, at least at this stage in his career, for catharsis and escape. To elude the conflicting, tormenting, and to some degree stultifying emotions of his own mind, he projects them into fictional protagonists who continually flutter between worlds of past and present, dreams and reali-

7. Carl Lefevre's valuable essay, "Lord Byron's Fiery Convert of Revenge," (*SP*, XLIX [1952], 468–487), is primarily an investigation of the hero figure in *Lara*; T. S. Eliot ("Byron," in *English Romantic Poets: Modern Essays in Criticism*, edited by M. H. Abrams [New York: Oxford University Press, 1960], pp. 196–209) briefly discusses *The Giaour*, but his interest is in narrative technique; and G. Wilson Knight ("The Two Eternities: An Essay on Byron," in *The Burning Oracle* [New York: Oxford University Press, 1939]) mentions imagery in the same poem but with biographical emphasis.

8. *The Letters and Journals of Lord Byron*, edited by Rowland E. Prothero, 6 vols. (London: John Murray, Ltd., 1898–1904), II, 278, hereafter cited as *L & J.*

9. *L & J*, II, 293; cf. II, 314.

10. *L & J*, II, 321.

11. *L & J*, III, 247; cf. III, 405; and V, 214–215. See also Meyer H. Abrams's analysis of the implications of this "psychic pressure" in *The Mirror and the Lamp* (New York: Oxford University Press, 1953), pp. 139ff.

ties, states of action and ennui, poles of passion and intellect. Although the dichotomies of Byron's nature are visible in those of his characters (and, to be sure, of all men), we should be careful to recognize the disparity between what Byron achieves by writing and what his protagonists fail to achieve in the narratives. The poet for the moment cures his lethargy, loses his "wretched identity," in the sheer excitement of writing.[12] In the process of expressing, chiefly through the images of these "dream poems," the irreconcilability of dreams and realities and the futility of seeking accord between the two, Byron temporarily disburdens himself of the misery which his own duality generates.

I

The Corsair[13] opens on Conrad, the pirate-captain, and his shipmates returning to their remote island port only to learn of an imminent attack from the Moslem Seyd. Determining to strike first, Conrad prepares for immediate embarkation, allowing himself a mere hour with his beloved Medora. His calloused nature only momentarily shaken by Medora's tears and forebodings, he sails at sunset and by dawn has slipped into a position of ambush.

Into Seyd's celebration of his expected victory, meanwhile, intrudes "a captive Dervise, from the pirate's nest" who reports Conrad's unpreparedness for battle. But while he speaks, fires from the Pacha's burning ships illuminate the court, the Dervise reveals himself as Conrad, and, as the pirates overrun the quarters, Seyd escapes. Conrad sets fire to the court but leads his pack to the Haram, bent on rescuing the slaves. After bearing Gulnare, Seyd's favorite, from the inferno, Conrad renews the battle, is wounded and imprisoned. Gulnare, having stolen Seyd's signet, gains admittance to Con-

---

12. See *L & J*, III, 400; V, 196 and 318.

13. I begin with *The Corsair* not so much because *The Giaour, The Bride of Abydos,* and Cantos I and II of *Childe Harold's Pilgrimage* have little to offer—though the first two are even cruder experiments in the genre than is *The Corsair*—but because the imagistic technique of *The Corsair* more clearly indicates the tack Byron takes and follows throughout the remainder of his career. All textual quotations are from Ernest Hartley Coleridge, editor, *The Poetical Works of Lord Byron*, 7 vols. (London: John Murray, Ltd., 1898–1904), III, 227–296, hereafter cited as *PW*.

rad's cell and promises to work for his escape. Medora, meanwhile, has fallen senseless after Conrad's failure to return.

After four days, Gulnare arrives at the cell with a plan and a poniard for the pirate, but Conrad refuses to wield a lady's weapon against Seyd. Gulnare therefore murders Seyd and takes Conrad to his waiting ship. Though repelled by her act, Conrad gratefully kisses Gulnare just before arriving home to discover Medora's darkened tower and the maiden herself dead. Broken by grief and guilt, Conrad disappears.

Primary among the difficulties of dealing with imagery in Byron's early verse is the poet's failure to make clear until near the end of a narrative what images should be regarded as central: that is, seldom is there a point at the outset by which to orient ourselves, a norm to serve as a standard from which a series of related images might draw their meanings. Marshall, overlooking such a standard, says of *The Corsair,* "the principal characters tend . . . to assume allegorical dimensions, largely representing either Love, Death, or a fusion of both."[14] Seyd, Medora, and Gulnare, certainly, represent Death, Love, and Love-Death respectively (as Marshall remarks); and among these three only Gulnare approaches credibility. But Conrad is altogether another matter: the whole tenor of the narrative seems to suggest that he, unlike Byron's earlier protagonists, is not a humanized abstraction; rather, his secondary attribute, "softness," offsets and diminishes the importance of his prevailing characteristic. If we conceive of the tale as an account of Conrad's quest for the realization or activation of this secondary quality, then the function of Medora, Gulnare, and the images associated with them becomes immediately clear. The theme of the piece is not so much the necessity for Conrad to reconcile love and death as it is his need to recognize the overwhelming force of emotional attachment in human life: he must be taught the meaning of love.

The imagistic norm for the poem is supplied by the following passage:

> His heart was formed for softness—warped to wrong,
> Betrayed too early, and beguiled too long;

14. P. 40.

Each feeling pure—as falls the dropping dew
Within the grot—like that hardened too;
Less clear, perchance, its earthly trials passed,
But sunk, and chilled, and petrified at last.
Yet tempests wear, and lightning cleaves the rock;
If such his heart, so shattered it the shock.
There grew one flower beneath its rugged brow,
Though dark the shade—it sheltered—saved till now.
The thunder came—that bolt hath blasted both,
The Granite's firmness, and the Lily's growth:
The gentle plant hath left no leaf to tell
Its tale, but shrunk and withered where it fell;
And of its cold protector, blacken round
But shivered fragments on the barren ground!
                    (III, xxiii, 1830–1845)

This is, of course, Conrad; and the dual poles of his nature—the masculine and feminine principles—are explicit in the diametrically opposed images of granite (associated with chilling, petrifaction, ruggedness, darkness) and the lily (suggesting softness, purity, growth, gentleness). But while the flower represents one penchant of Conrad's character, it simultaneously symbolizes the fragile and inviolate Medora, who is, probably, a physical embodiment of the "tender" features of the hero. She is in fact the first of Byron's many counterpart figures—most notably personified later in Astarte and Adah. "Granite" and "lily," at any rate, are coexistent qualities in the same being, and although the first substantially overbalances the second in importance through the poem, the "withering" of Medora ironically forces upon Conrad a kind of emotional salvation; for in suffering her loss, his own "granite" nature dissolves like dew. Clearly, he is no longer "exempt / From all affection and from all contempt." His practice of retreating into military engagements in moments of emotional stress, of searching there for a meaningful and profitable existence, has been exposed to him as an empty and futile effort.

But if Conrad the rock is softened by the tenderness of Medora, Conrad the man of fire is equally chilled by the cold treachery of Gulnare. The Corsair's "dark eyebrow shades a glance of fire;" he is possessed by a "burning spirit;" and the flash of lightning is "To him more genial than the midnight star." Confronted with Gulnare's murder of Seyd, however,

> From all his feelings in their inmost force—
> So thrilled, so shuddered every creeping vein,
> As now they froze before that purple stain.
>   (III, x, 1591–1593)

And Gulnare, for her part, "watched his features till she could not bear / Their freezing aspect." But a Medora-like tenderness, a countenance "changed and humbled," "faint and meek," a hand "So soft in love," in Gulnare eventually warm Conrad to a recognition of her love and sacrifice on his behalf, and motivate his reluctant gesture of gratitude. The steadfastness of the slave-queen and her eagerness to risk all for love prepare Conrad psychologically for the staggering impact of Medora's sacrifice.

The Corsair's humanitarian warming toward Gulnare occurs too late for his emotional redemption in the eyes of Medora; and in an ironic reversal of his major images, Byron now presents the maiden in death, with "cold flowers [in] her colder hand contained," with dark lashes fringing "lids of snow." The compression of the latter metaphor is remarkable in a poem so uniformly prolix, for in it Byron has juxtaposed the qualities of the lily (fragility, purity, beauty) against the numb chill of death.[15] In any event, the meaning of Medora's death is not lost upon Conrad: he cannot but blame himself for disregarding his own and Medora's premonitions about his battle with Seyd, or for underestimating the authority of emotion. Whereas his heart had formerly been the sheltered crevice in which the flower flourished, it now becomes a "cold protector" of the "shrunk and withered" plant. His pride is in shambles, and his guilt at last has cause.

From an imagistic point of view, The Corsair is relatively shabby. What figures appear are stereotyped, crude, and usually thin, and only scanty evidence indicates a serious interest in the potentialities of thematic imagery. But the central configuration of the poem does

15. For this reading I am indebted to Clement Tyson Goode, "Byron's Early Romances: A Study," Unpublished Ph.D. Dissertation, Vanderbilt University, 1959, p. 323.

depict the duality of Conrad's character; and in view of what happens with imagery in *Lara* and *Parisina,* one may conclude that Byron uses the device here in a trial-and-error fashion in order to determine whether it may contribute anything useful to his poetry.

I I

The plot of *Lara*[16] is deceptively simple. The "long self-exiled chieftain," Lara, returns with a page, Kaled, to his kingdom where only their lord's silence and haughty demeanor prevents the serfs from a joyful celebration. One midnight in the castle a shriek brings servants to the portrait gallery where Lara lies senseless, a sword by his side and a curse on his lips. Later, at the ball of a neighboring lord, Otho, Lara encounters a certain Sir Ezzelin who hints openly about an ugly secret in Lara's past; but at Otho's intervention, the two agree to settle the altercation at an assembly next morning. After Ezzelin fails to appear at court, Lara wounds Otho in a duel over Ezzelin's honor. Now anticipating open warfare, Lara frees his vassals and rallies them to his support but in the showdown with Otho is soundly defeated. He expires in the arms of Kaled (who, it turns out, is his disguised lover) and is buried on the battlefield. Distracted with grief, Kaled dies at the graveside. An unidentified peasant claims to have seen a horseman cast what looked like a body into a nearby river on the night of Ezzelin's disappearance.

No doubt Byron drew heavily upon certain eighteenth-century sources[17] for the elements of mystery in which *Lara* is clothed, but he uses these stereotyped materials to a thematic purpose which clearly transcends their mechanical employment in the earlier works. Especially important in this connection is the function of the dream-image, possibly the central figure in the poem. With Lara's initial

16. Byron suggests in the "Advertisement" to *Lara* that the poem may be seen as a sequel to *The Corsair,* reintroducing Gulnare as the Page and Conrad as the titular hero. However that may be, interest in motive, total characterization, and thematic imagery is considerably more evident here than in the former piece.

17. For a discussion of these matters, see Bertrand Evans, *Gothic Drama From Walpole to Shelley* (Berkeley: University of California Press, 1947); Ernest J. Lovell, Jr., *Byron: The Record of a Quest* (Austin: University of Texas Press, 1949), pp. 117–184; and Thorslev, *passim.*

reappearance, for example, his entire kingdom acquires illusionary features: inhabitants still "see . . . recognize, yet almost deem / The present dubious, or the past a dream." Lara's experiences in exile—whatever they were—have forced him to awaken "from the wildness of that dream" of youth. After the hero's paroxysm in the portrait gallery, Kaled attempts to "soothe away the horrors of his dream— / If dream it were . . . / What'er his frenzy dreamed or eye beheld;" "Was it a dream?" the poet reiterates, and offers no answer. "A thing of dark imaginings" whose "early dreams outstripped the truth," Lara is as much victimized by his own nightmarish fantasies as by the supposed treachery of his calumniators. We are warned ominously after Ezzelin's appearance that "there are things which we must dream and dare, / And execute ere thought be half aware." And as Lara leaves the ballroom,

> all bosoms seem
> To bound as doubting from too black a dream,
> Such as we know is false, yet dread in sooth,
> Because the worst is ever nearest truth.
> (I, xxviii, 620–623)

Canto I closes with a brief meditation on the blessed relief of sleep, especially that which "dreams the least."

As I have suggested, most of the alarming and conjectural events of the narrative occur in moonlight, or shadowy half-light, which of course intensifies the mysteriousness they are meant primarily to convey. For instance, "as the moonbeam shone / Through the lattice o'er the floor of stone," Lara's

> bristling locks of sable, brow of gloom,
> And the wide waving of his shaken plume,
> Glanced like a spectre's attributes . . . .
> (I, xi, 197–199)

Ezzelin, moreover, with his dark hints of some damaging secret, resembles "a meteor of the night / Who menaced but to disappear with light." Deceptive, cunning, "consenting Night / Guides with her star" Lara's counterattack against Otho, and leads the hero's forces directly into an ambush. Moonlight transforms Kaled's usually fiery countenance into an aspect of "unwonted hue / Of mournful paleness, whose deep tint expressed / The truth, and not the terror of his breast." Finally, the peasant's alleged observation of the horseman's disposal of a body occurred "When Cynthia's light almost gave way to morn / And nearly veiled in mist her waning horn."

An appropriate corollary to these images of dim or refracted light is the frequent description of Lara's present demeanor in figures of "coldness," often as opposed to his former fervently passionate bearing. For example, he retains "The pride, but not the fire, of early days," and his chief trait now is a "Coldness of mien." Discovered unconscious in the gallery, he appears "Cold as the marble where his length was laid, / Pale as the beam that o'er his features played;" the metaphorical association of coldness with moonlight is explicit. His "fiery passions" having "poured their wrath / In hurried desolation o'er his path," he now "coldly" bypasses mankind, for his blood in "icy smoothness" flows. "With all that chilling mystery of mien," that "accent cold," he provides a striking contrast to Kaled, who, because of the repeated descriptions of her in fire and heat imagery, is surely meant symbolically to represent Lara's former self. The hero awaits the appearance of Ezzelin with a "coldly patient air," and later, his weaponed hand speaks with an "almost careless coolness." Suitably enough, in the final scene, "Kaled will not part / With the cold grasp" of her expiring lover.

The essential function of these dream, moonlight, and ice images, however, does not become clear until they are contrasted with images of sun, dawn, and unobstructed light. Two passages, one opening Canto II and the other appearing near the end of the poem, are crucial:

> Night wanes—the vapours round the mountains curled
> Melt into morn, and Light awakes the world.
>
> . . . .
>
> But mighty Nature bounds as from her birth,
> The Sun is in the heavens, and Life on earth;
> Flowers in the valley, splendour in the beam,
> Health on the gale, and freshness in the stream.
>
> (II, i, 646–647; 650–653)

In this heavily ironic prelude to imminent calamity, Byron simultaneously pictures the unsullied beauties of Nature revealed by the rising sun, and imagistically foreshadows the following passage:

> But from his [Lara's] visage little could we guess,
> So unrepentant—dark—and passionless,
> Save that when struggling nearer to his last,
> Upon that page his eye was kindly cast;
> And once, as Kaled's answering accents ceased,
> Rose Lara's hand, and pointed to the East:
> Whether (as then the breaking Sun from high
> Rolled back the clouds) the morrow caught his eye,
> Or that 'twas chance—or some remembered scene,
> That raised his arm to point where such had been,
> Scarce Kaled seemed to know, but turned away,
> As if his heart abhorred that coming day,
> And shrunk his glance before that morning light,
> To look on Lara's brow—where all grew night.
>   (II, xix, 1107–1120)

Together the two passages provide the imagistic norm for the poem, for each represents, with differing emphasis, the coming of the light, the dissipation of darkness, and, in the second quotation, its effect upon the characters involved. Although the cause for Lara's action, and even its exact import, remain vague, Byron attempts to illustrate through the imagery here a kind of spiritual rebirth in the hero. Still "unrepentant," Lara nevertheless indulges in a "kindly" gesture toward Kaled—his first in the poem toward anyone—and his figurative association with the East, the rising sun, and the dissolving clouds carries overtones of at least a momentary regeneration. If we assume that Lara's symbolic relation to refracted light indicates his guilt, or sin, or, simply, the secretive side of his character, then his symbolic relation to unobstructed light in these final lines may suggest an expiation of his crime or a conversion of his character.

The specific nature of Lara's crime, as is usual with Byron's protagonists, remains inscrutable, but he is clearly "guilty" on several counts, all of which can perhaps be reduced to the deadly sin of pride. In youth he was primarily a creature of "feelings," "burning for pleasure," "all action and all life," who turned to "intenseness" as an "escape from thought." But during his exile, something occurred which tamed the wildness of his character, "withered" his heart, and cast him into a chronic state of despondency. Consequently, he tends to dwell excessively on the past[18] and he fails to reconcile the opposing inclinations of his being toward "feeling" and "thought:" that is, youthful *feeling* convinced Lara that somewhere a lofty and attainable ideal toward which man should strive encouraged and sustained him in that effort; but adult *thought* has proved that "His early dreams of good outstripped the truth," and he is now confronted with the "thought of years in phantom chase misspent." Thought, truth, and the present, therefore, press upon Lara the necessity of accepting a fairly bleak reality, while feelings, dreams, and the past still fortify his faith in an ideal. Hence, "his mind would half exult and half regret" its youthful indulgence. Such a duality of character cannot of course be construed as a crime, but the irreconcilability of the two impulses both accounts in large part for Lara's guilt feelings and clearly motivates what *are* crimes.

The first offense is Lara's refusal to accept responsibility for the apparent worthlessness of his life:

> He called on Nature's self to share the shame,
> And charged all faults upon the fleshly form
> She gave to clog the soul, and feast the worm;
> Till he at last confounded good and ill,
> And half mistook for fate the acts of will.
> (I, xviii, 332–336)

Pride, "some strange perversity of thought," and a fundamental fear of being held accountable for any act motivate Lara's disclaimer and his accusation of Nature. This familiar Byronic formula is of course a complementary adjunct to the dream-reality theme: it is after all the conflict between the aspiring spirit and the clogging body which withers Lara's heart.

Be that as it may, Lara's pride manifests itself in other ways as well. Endowed "With more capacity for love than earth / Bestows on most of mortal mould and birth," Lara has either exhausted that capacity in the foreign country or consciously repressed it. Nowhere

18. Note particularly I, 181–234; and II, 1090–1098.

does he show the slightest love interest in Kaled—perhaps for security reasons, but more likely because he no longer trusts the responses of the heart: in self-protection he stiffens himself against any
affective stimuli. How then should we explain his attachment to the
page? Again the imagery is helpful. Kaled hails from a climate where
"the soul glows beneath a brighter star;" of a frail form, he has a
"darkly delicate . . . brow whereon his native sun had sate." His
frequent blush reveals "a hectic tint"

> That for a burning moment fevered there;
> And the wild sparkle of his eye seemed caught
> From high, and lightened with electric thought.
>   (I, xxvi, 535–537)

He is marked by a "latent fierceness that far more became / His
fiery climate than his tender frame." And after Lara's death, Kaled's
"eye shot forth with . . . living fire." The page's characterization in
heat and fire figures—note especially allusions to the sun—are meant
to show his similarity to the young Lara; hence, the hero has ever by
him a mirror of his own youth on which he can dote with self-pitying
nostalgia. Again obvious is Lara's unwillingness to give up the past,
to reconcile himself to the immediate responsibilities of life, to abandon a futile—though by now only half-hearted—quest for ideal
existence.

One might argue that Lara becomes reconciled to the necessity for
benevolent action as a cure for ennui and retrospection, for he does
emancipate his vassals and revel with them in a celebration of their
freedom. Moreover, we learn that beggars and other social unfortu-
nates found sympathetic asylum at Lara's gate: "For them, at least,
his soul compassion knew. / Cold to the great, contemptuous to the
high, / The humble passed not his unheeding eye." But such benevo-
lence is merely utilitarian posturing: "What cared he for the freedom
of the crowd? / He raised the humble but to bend the proud." He
acts to the last not out of compassion or a sense of duty, but in
retaliation for his wounded pride against any and all opposition: an
ego which has aspired to perfection and been shattered by a half-
recognition of imperfection in itself attempts to find satisfaction by
destroying whatever semblance of stature or stability others possess.
And Lara employs the most devious means to that end.

Still, as I have said, a kind of spiritual or emotional conversion is depicted in Lara's gesture toward Kaled and the blaze of sun in the East. Physically, of course, Lara endures humiliating defeat; but in his recognition of and gratitude for Kaled's loyalty, and in his last-minute effort to incorporate into himself, as it were, the energy, the heat, the intensity of the rising sun, there momentarily appears a residual spark of the youthful, promising, passionate Lara whose energies for genuine achievement were somehow enervated by his failure to accept the imperfection of human nature. His appearance within the narrative should perhaps be viewed as an eclipse bracketed by sunlight, ardor, and strength of character. If not altogether dead, the battery of Lara's passions clearly needs recharging; and in his culminating struggle with Otho—where, significantly, "Himself he spared not"—though his motives are ignoble, a certain diminution of his pride and a participation in action for its own sake suggest at least an instantaneous achievement of his goal. At the moment of his seeming triumph—"once they seemed to fly— / Now was the time, he waved his hand on high"—an arrow pierces "the unguarded side." In an instant of absolute self-negation, of self-loss in commitment to the battle, Lara wins the right to claim, at the last, kinship with the sun.

Lara's fleeting regeneration, however, cannot be considered religiously orthodox in any sense, for immediately after his metaphorical identification with the sun, he glances with an "eye profane" upon a proffered "absolving cross." The gesture is of course typically Byronic, for the disenchanted Calvinist in the poet will not permit him to represent any sort of religious capitulation in a soul which has lived in staunchly maintained defiance of any source of philosophic or theological support other than that provided by itself. Lara's disdainful rebuff of the "holy beads" is not so much a climactic act of pride as it is a refusal to surrender an independence which has endowed him with the courage to face death fearlessly. Any belief in the efficacy of Christian paraphernalia would render meaningless his previous reconciliation with the natural universe.

III

Parisina, Byron notes in his "Advertisement" to the tale, is based upon an account in Gibbon's *Miscellaneous Works:* ". . . the Marquis of Este discovered the incestuous loves of his wife Parisina, and Hugo his bastard son, a beautiful and valiant youth. They were beheaded in the castle by the sentence of a father and husband, who published his shame, and survived their execution."[19] Byron alters his source in these particulars: Hugo accuses Azo (his father) of brutality toward Bianca (his mother), Parisina survives Hugo's execution and mysteriously disappears, and Azo sires more sons by another wife but lives on in grief-stricken wretchedness.

The imputations of Parisina's attendants, Marshall believes,

> establish for Azo as fact the possibility which, though consciously torturing him, unconsciously gratifies his need for a seemingly rational basis for his attribution of his own sense of guilt to Hugo. . . . mixed with Hugo's conscious grief at Parisina's plight is an unconscious satisfaction at the pain which he has caused Azo, who, he feels, has wronged him by transferring to him his own image of guilt. . . . Hugo's assumption of the possession of the axe, the instrument to be used in his execution, is the means by which he symbolizes the completion of his victory over his father, his revenge for what he feels is the cause of the death of his mother and for his own humiliation, which can end only in his own death. . . . [Hugo] sees himself sacrificed not as the agent but as the victim of his father. . . . identifying himself with his father, Hugo unconsciously assumes the place of the father in the reconstructed relationship with Bianca, of which the affair with Parisina has been in part a symbol, a re-enactment.[20]

This perceptive reading solves several major problems raised by the narrative, but at the same time it introduces new complications. For one thing, it tends to reduce the titular character to a passive weapon manipulated by Azo and Hugo respectively in their "unconscious" conflict: stripped of any unique individuality, she becomes merely the victim in their psychological warfare. Second, Marshall disproportionately emphasizes Hugo's attachment to his mother, for in contrast to that relationship, his incestuous affair with Parisina pales to near irrelevancy. Third, Marshall does not stress as strongly as the tale warrants the depth of Azo's affection for his wife and son, and the eventual chaos of emotions which besets the prince. Finally, since

19. *PW*, III, 503.
20. Pp. 64–66.

Marshall is not concerned primarily with imagery (beyond the symbolic import of the axe), he mistakes, I think, the very crux of the poem, which is not the execution of Hugo but Azo's consequential failure to reconcile the justice of his act with his parental and marital love: his failure, that is, to harmonize head with heart, thought with feeling. True, the poem treats crime, guilt, and retribution, and all three sinners, perhaps, get their proper rewards; but Azo suffers most severely, for not only has he paid with blood for his offense against Bianca, but now he must live with the suspicion that his participation in the fates of Hugo and Parisina was an even grosser crime against nature and love.

The setting for Parisina's and Hugo's illicit liaison contrasts ironically with the lovers' attitude toward their affair. They meet at twilight in a lush, heavily-wooded grove where "gentle winds, and water near, / Make music," where "full-blown" flowers, leaves, waves, and a "foliage thick"—all symbols of Nature's dynamic richness and vitality—converge in paradisiacal fertility. But Parisina and Hugo are oblivious to this co-operation and encouragement on the part of Nature:

> And what to them is the world beside,
> With all its change of time and tide?
> Its living things—its earth and sky—
> Are nothing to their mind and eye.
> And heedless as the dead are they
>   Of aught around, above, beneath;
> As if all else had passed away,
>   They only for each other breathe . . . .
>   (ll. 29–36)

In one sense, Hugo and Parisina are already dead, for their moral irresponsibility, their denial of all former commitments and obligations, and particularly their effort to exempt themselves from the "change of time and tide," have a stagnating, if not killing, effect. Their obsession with each other, of course, guarantees a momentary release from the anguish of guilt; but their attempt, like Juan's and Haidée's later, to construct a universe governed by an inflexible law of passionate indulgence is destined to failure by the very nature of human character. It is but another example in Byron's works of people trying to transcend and deny the flux of mortal life by relocating themselves in some imagined paradise of permanence. Byron is scrupulous to point out the futility of such endeavors: as though from an enchanting dream, he notes, "we must awake before / We know such vision comes no more."

Parisina and Hugo depart the "spot of guilty gladness" with the consciousness of their sin—"The deep and shuddering chill"—heavy upon them, and in a matter of minutes, Parisina, muttering in her "fevered" sleep, reveals the identity of her paramour. Azo's initial impulse is to stab Parisina where she lies, but "He could not slay a thing so fair— / At least not smiling, sleeping there." Even in the fury of his discovery, Azo cannot subdue the passion of his heart long enough to commit an act for which he apparently has every legal justification. Not a rational preference to await confirmation of Parisina's guilt but the hypnotic force of her beauty stays the hand of the prince.

With a rapidity designed to shorten the duration of his misery, Azo summons the guilty pair before the assembled court. But his speech of indictment—in tone, childishly whimpering, in logic, rationalized and equivocating—betrays a fundamental uncertainty concerning the moral justice of the order he must issue (ll. 198–222). Of more significance, however, is Azo's reference to his marital and parental bond as "That dream [which] this morning passed away." The prince, I think, has attempted to obscure his own sense of shame over the Bianca affair by fabricating a domestic paradise with Hugo and Parisina, but has by their incestuous act been sharply reminded that the claims of the flesh cannot always be deferred to the ideals of the spirit. At any rate, Azo finally pronounces the death-sentence, condemns Parisina to "view the head" of her lover, and disclaims his own responsibility for Hugo's fate: "Not I, but thou [Parisina] his blood dost shed." Having performed with only limited success his duty as judge, prince, cuckolded husband, and shamed parent, Azo "hid his face,"

> For on his brow the swelling vein
> Throbbed as if back upon his brain,
> The hot blood ebbed and flowed again;

> And therefore bowed he for a space,
> And passed his shaking hand along
> His eye to veil it from the throng.
>
> (ll. 224–229)

The image of blood heated to the boiling point is here fused with and qualified by the sea metaphor, the first image representing the fury of Azo's wrath[21] but the second figuring his inability to sustain passionate rage: as a unit, the image presents with considerable force and vividness the confusion of Azo's emotions.

The emphasis of Hugo's long speech (ll. 234–317) is not so much upon Azo's neglect and mistreatment of Bianca and her son as it is upon the physical and temperamental inheritance which the prince bequeathed Hugo. In "lineaments," in "spirit," in "this tamelessness of heart," in his "arm of strength" and "soul of flame" are evidenced the distinguishing characteristics of the father. Conscious that he shares an identity of spirit with Azo, the son pointedly hints that he has, with Parisina, acted only according to the tradition established by the father: "I am no bastard in my soul, / For that, like thine, abhorred control." Azo's "guilty love" has repaid him with "too like a son!" Concentration here should focus upon allusions to tamelessness, impetuosity, recklessness where matters of the heart are involved: ironically, only after Hugo is physically bound can he speak freely about the cause for his crime. And Azo "starts" (l. 289) not because his psychological motives have been found out by Hugo, but because he clearly perceives, first of all, the identity of Hugo's sin with his own, and, more important, the futility of imposing rigid strictures of conduct on hearts governed exclusively by passion. Furthermore, as it turns out, Azo's own moral wantonness was not limited to the Bianca affair: twice in his speech Hugo reminds his father that the prince, coveting Parisina's charms, stole his son's "destined bride." Azo's ethical debility is thus heavily underscored, as is his hypocrisy in endeavoring to judge Hugo according to a law which he himself has not upheld.

In marked contrast to the warm, loving Parisina of stanzas ii and

21. See Goode, p. 323.

iii but extending the image of the "iciness" of detected guilt (the "shuddering chill" of line 63), the "heroine" now stands before the court "with glassy gaze . . . / As ice were in her curdled blood." Attempting to speak, she can utter only "one long shriek,"

> And to the earth she fell like stone
> Or statue from its base o'er thrown,
> More like a thing that n'er had life,—
> A monument of Azo's wife,—
> Than her, that living guilty thing,
> Whose every passion was a sting,
> Which urged to guilt, but could not bear
> That guilt's detection and despair.
>
> (ll. 348–355)

The two opposing tendencies of Parisina's character are presented explicitly here in the statuesque and "stinging" images: on the one hand she can be coldly rational in the knowledge that physical promiscuity entails deception and remorse,[22] while on the other hand a stinging, unrestrainable impulse commits her to profligacy despite the correspondent guilt which it invariably evokes. Emptied of passion she is stony, deathlike, adamant; but the proper impetus, such as Hugo, can stimulate her enormous capacities for passionate indulgence. Parisina, then, within the metaphorical construct of the poem, is the feminine complement to the duality of Azo's character, for he is no more subject than she to the dominion of mind over heart. And with perfect consistency Byron shows that her effort to subjugate passion to reason precipitates the collapse of her mental faculties: she

> all too soon
> Recovered from that death-like swoon,
> But scarce to reason—every sense
> Had been o'erstrung by pangs intense
>
> . . . .
>
> All was confused and undefined
> To her all-jarred and wandering mind;
> A chaos of wild hopes and fears.
> And now in laughter, now in tears,

22. See also ll. 63, 368–369, 427, 480, 534, and 550–556.

> But madly still in each extreme,
> She strove with that convulsive dream;
> For so it seemed on her to break—
> Oh! vainly must she strive to wake!
>   (ll. 356–359; 378–385)

One may observe in passing, too, Parisina's subconscious desire to recapture the idyllic dreaminess of her affair with Hugo, her hesitation to accept the present reality as anything but a horrible nightmare.

Now the sun, with its imagistic associations of fire and energy, ironically appears to rebuke the trio for their attempts to deny or conceal the force of their passions. It "rose upon that heavy day / And moved it with his steadiest ray;" presently, "his evening beams are shed / Full on Hugo's fated head. / . . . That high sun on his head did glisten, / . . . But brighter still the beam was thrown / Upon the axe which near him shone / With a clear and ghastly glitter." The double metaphorical emphasis upon the juxtaposition of sun and head draws attention once again to the thought-emotion paradox. By representing the sun gleaming more brightly upon the axe—the image, Marshall notes, of rational authority and justice—Byron seems to accent the error of Azo's decision to destroy the love of Parisina and Hugo.

Beyond the assurance that Parisina goes mad with grief, we learn nothing of her fate. But Azo lives on in misery, marked by "Scars of the lacerating mind / Which the Soul's war doth leave behind." Presumably, the rage of conflicting elements within his psyche leaves him shattered but by no means immune to thought or feeling. Although his heart shuns itself, he can neither "yield" to a recognition of the legal justice of his decision, nor "forget" the emotional injustice of it. In a telling image, Byron notes that Azo's heart,

> when it least appeared to melt,
> Intensely thought, intensely felt;
> The deepest ice which ever froze
> Can only o'er the surface close;
> The living stream lies quick below,
> And flows—and cannot cease to flow.
>   (ll. 551–556)

The battle of the dualities continues "intensely;" Azo achieves no reconciliation between the opposing tendencies of his character. But at least he has been brought to a recognition of them, perhaps to a realization that thought and feeling never operate independently in a vacuum but perpetually interact upon each other, and that human conduct cannot be governed by a strict enforcement of either alone. That supposition is confirmed by Byron's epigrammatic tag to the poem:

> The tainted branches of a tree,
>   If lopped with care, a strength may give,
>   By which the rest shall bloom and live
> All greenly fresh and wildly free:
> But if the lightning, in its wrath,
> The waving boughs with fury scathe,
> The massy trunk the ruin feels,
> And never more a leaf reveals.[23]
>   (ll. 579–586)

Framed symbolically in terms of vegetative growth, reproduction, and continuity respectively opposed to disease, sterility, and destruction, the passage encapsulates the point that Azo has sacrificed himself, his son, and his wife by failing, in the first case, to accept the moral responsibility for indiscriminately indulged passion, and, in the second, to temper with humanitarian mercy the rigid implementation of the law. To obey exclusively the dictates of either thought or feeling, Byron's total poetic statement seems to say, is to invite disaster; to co-ordinate them in a harmonious relationship is to forge a life "All greenly fresh and wildly free."

If we recall at this point Byron's awkward and stereotyped application of floral and stone figures in support of characterization in *The Corsair,* we may remark that his early effort has matured, with *Lara* and *Parisina,* into a relatively sophisticated use of imagery, not only to fortify characterization and theme, but also to bear much of the weight of communication in the poetry. The three central dream,

---

23. One must concede that Byron's use of "lightning" here is totally at variance with his pattern of imagery throughout *Parisina,* as well as with his characterization of Azo as a ruler whose fury is radically cooled by affection for his son and wife.

light, and cold configurations are neatly brought together and reconciled in Lara's final "awakening," and the paradoxes of character in *Parisina* are from first to last indicated through the imagery. Few of Byron's images, of course, are original or unique; nor is his procedural method particularly subtle. But the assumption that the poet has by early 1816 recognized the utility of thematic imagery is borne out by the recurrence and refinement of the metaphorical patterns examined above in *The Prisoner of Chillon,* Canto III of *Childe Harold's Pilgrimage,* and *Manfred.*

The Elemental Chaos

It is an awful chaos—light and darkness,
And mind and dust, and passions and pure thoughts,
Mixed, and contending without end or order,
All dormant or destructive.

—Manfred

ON 2 January 1815 Lord Byron wed Annabella Milbanke. Almost exactly a year later this priggish woman, with their infant daughter, left the poet; and on 25 April 1816 Byron sailed for the continent. Arriving in Switzerland by way of the Rhine, he established lodgings on the banks of Lake Geneva and soon became an intimate associate of Shelley, Mary Wollstonecraft Godwin, and, inescapably, Claire Clairmont. In the fall of the same year he toured the Alps. *The Prisoner of Chillon* and *Childe Harold's Pilgrimage,* Canto III, were completed in June 1816 and the revised version of *Manfred* in July 1817. During these fourteen months the poet considered himself an exile.

Never in Byron's experience was the contention between the opposing tendencies of his thought more severe than during his sojourn in Switzerland. Even under the powerful influence of Shelley and, through him, Wordsworth, reconciliation of fundamental dichotomies was only temporarily approximated, for Byron's skepticism was rather more increased than diminished by the uncompromising certitude with which Shelley propounded Wordsworth's doctrines of natural harmony and benevolent necessity. Certainly, Wordsworth and Shelley are clearly visible in Byron's poems of this period; through some of them throbs a yearning for the kind of placid synthesis which regulates much of Wordsworth's verse. But at the same time Byron shrinks from the belief that Wordsworth's and Shelley's truth is *final* truth, that observation and assimilation of natural beauty provide the means for reconciling oneself to the contradictions of human experience. "*Almost* thou persuadest me," Byron might have

said to Shelley, for he wishes quite desperately to believe; and, indeed, at times his skepticism gets momentarily clouded by what at
first glance appear to be pantheistic deifications of Nature. But Byron
always thumps himself back soundly to a recognition of the futility
and even the danger of such self-deceiving dreams—to an understanding, that is, that the beauties of Nature are invariably "lost on a
soul so constituted"[1] of fire and clay, spirit and matter, emotion and
intellect. Whatever of Wordsworth and Shelley informs these poems
is filtered through and radically tempered by the Byronic notion that
life is first and last a wild and shapeless "chaos of the elements."

Because this "Wordsworthian note"[2] is peculiarly connected with
the imagery of Byron's 1816–1817 works, it is instructive to pause
here over various comments by the poet and others on the extent of
Shelley's influence. Thomas Medwin reports a conversation on the
subject:

I said to him, "You are accused of owing a great deal to Wordsworth.
Certainly there are some stanzas in the Third Canto of 'Childe Harold'
that smell strongly of the Lakes. . . ." "Very possibly," replied he.
"Shelley, when I was in Switzerland, used to dose me with Wordsworth
physic even to nausea; and I do remember then reading some things of
his with pleasure. He had once a feeling of Nature, which he carried
almost to a deification of it:—that's why Shelley liked his poetry."[3]

Wordsworth himself, however, did not view the matter with quite so
much detachment: he "spoke of Byron's plagiarisms from him; the

---

1. Byron's 1813 "Addition to the Preface" of *Childe Harold's Pilgrimage,*
Cantos I and II, in *The Poetical Works of Lord Byron,* edited by Ernest
Hartley Coleridge, 7 vols. (London: John Murray, Ltd., 1898–1904), II, 8; all
textual references are to this edition, hereafter cited as *PW.*

2. Ernest J. Lovell, Jr. (*Byron: The Record of a Quest* [Austin: University
of Texas Press, 1949]) suggests that the "Wordsworthian note" is an expression of Byron's *mobilité,* "acted upon by others and reflecting views wholly
foreign to his more usual thoughts and feelings" (p. 117). My debt to Professor Lovell's excellent discussion will be obvious in the following paragraphs.
The general drift of our arguments is identical, but in some particulars,
emphases and conclusions are different. In any event, readers interested in
pursuing the subject should consult Chapter V of Lovell's book.

3. *Medwin's Conversations of Lord Byron,* edited by Ernest J. Lovell, Jr.
(Princeton: Princeton University Press, 1966), p. 194.

whole third canto of 'Childe Harold' founded on his style and sentiments. The feeling of natural objects which is there expressed, not
caught by B. from nature herself, but from him [Wordsworth], and
spoiled in the transmission. 'Tintern Abbey' the source of it all."[4]
Both statements are probably exaggerated. Everybody knows that
Byron wearied of his efforts to locate consolation in Nature and that,
late in life, he irascibly repudiated Shelley's earlier evangelical attempts to reshape his philosophy along neo-Platonic lines. But more
than a grain of truth inhabits Wordsworth's remark. Having no encompassing *Weltanschauung* of his own and only half-believing in
Shelleyan and Wordsworthian sentiments concerning Nature, Byron
sought to convince himself of their validity by mimicry: perhaps by
writing like those authors he could come to think and feel as they
did. Byron was of course profoundly stirred by the natural beauty of
Geneva and the surrounding Alps: he must not be accused of mere
histrionic attitudinizing in the poems of this period. We should recognize, however, that his "mystical" communions with Nature were
bleakly frustrating spiritual experiences, supplying him with neither
an insight into absolute truth nor more than an instantaneous relief
from the sense of his own "wretched identity." He was sincerely
striving toward a union with the Great Whole; that he failed to
achieve it is simply another example of his awareness of the human
dilemma.

Critics are often disposed to quote passages from the Third Canto
of *Childe Harold's Pilgrimage* in support of a contention that Byron
did shake off his mortality long enough to merge with some "great
principle" of the universe.[5] A more convincing proof of this view is
Byron's note to the ninety-ninth stanza of *Childe Harold*, Canto III:

the feeling with which all around Clarens, and the opposite rocks of Meil-
lerie, is invested, is of a higher and more comprehensive order than the
mere sympathy with individual passion; it is a sense of the existence of
love in its most extended and sublime capacity, and of our own participation of its good and of its glory: it is the great principle of the universe,

4. Thomas Moore, *Memoirs, Journal and Correspondence of Thomas
Moore,* edited by Lord John Russell, 8 vols. (London: Longman, Green and
Co., Ltd., 1853–1856), III, 161.
5. For example, stanzas lxxxi–lxxv, xc, xciii, c–cii.

which is there more condensed, but not less manifested; and of which, though knowing ourselves a part, we lose our individuality, and mingle in the beauty of the whole.[6]

This of course might be Rousseau,[7] and it details the kind of "romantic" experience familiar in Wordsworth's and Shelley's verse. But now compare with this *public* statement Byron's descriptions of other impressive natural phenomena in *private* letters to Augusta Leigh:[8]

Arrived at the foot of the Mountain (the Yung frau, *i.e.*, the Maiden); Glaciers, torrents; one of these torrents *nine hundred feet* in height of visible descent . . . heard an Avalanche fall, like thunder; . . . all in perfection, and beautiful . . . The torrent is in shape curving over the rock, like the *tail* of a white horse streaming in the wind, such as it might be conceived would be that of the *"pale"* horse on which *Death* is mounted in the Apocalypse. It is neither mist nor water, but a something between both; it's [*sic*] immense height (nine hundred feet) gives it a wave, a curve, a spreading here, a condensation there, wonderful and indescribable.[9]

On the next evening he recorded:

Before ascending the mountain, went to the torrent (7 in the morning) again; the Sun upon it forming a *rainbow* of the lower part of all colours, but principally purple and gold; the bow moving as you move; I never saw anything like this; it is only in the Sunshine. . . . Heard the Avalanches falling every five minutes nearby—as if God was pelting the

6. *PW*, II, 304–305.

7. See Byron's letter to John Murray, 27 June 1816: "I have traversed all Rousseau's ground, with the *Heloise* before me; and am struck, to a degree, with the force and accuracy of his descriptions, and the beauty of their reality" (*The Letters and Journals of Lord Byron*, edited by Rowland E. Prothero, 6 vols. [London: John Murray, Ltd., 1898–1904], III, 335; hereafter cited as *L & J*).

8. The tour Byron recounts in this journal to Augusta did not begin until 18 September 1816, not quite three months after the completion of *Childe Harold's Pilgrimage*, Canto III. The poet's letters written between his arrival on the continent and the beginning of this journal contain almost no descriptive passages beyond some bitter carping about the foul weather. It is fair to assume, I think, that Byron's attitude toward Nature had not altered significantly, if at all, in the interim.

9. *L & J*, III, 357–358.

Devil down from Heaven with snow balls. . . . the clouds rose from the opposite valley, curling up perpendicular precipices like the foam of the Ocean of Hell, during a Springtide—it was white, and sulphury, and immeasurably deep in appearance. . . . on arriving at the summit, we looked down the other side upon a boiling sea of cloud, dashing against the crags on which we stood (these crags on one side quite perpendicular). . . . In passing the masses of snow, I made a snowball and pelted H[obhouse] with it. . . . rode to the higher Glacier—twilight, but distinct—very fine Glacier, like *a frozen hurricane.* Starlight, beautiful, but a devil of a path! . . . a little lightning; but the whole of the day as fine in point of weather as the day on which Paradise was made. Passed *whole woods of withered pines, all withered;* trunks stripped and barkless, branches lifeless; done by a single winter,—their appearance reminded me of me and my family.[10]

In two letters to John Murray (29 and 30 September 1816) Byron repeats the height and depth specifications and the "Ocean of Hell" figure, and then adds significantly:

I have been to Clarens . . . and crossed the mountains behind it: of this tour I kept a short journal for Mrs. Leigh, which I sent yesterday in three letters. It is not at all for perusal; but if you like to hear about the romantic part, she will, I dare say, show you what touches upon the rocks, etc., but it has not—nor can have anything to do with publication.[11]

To this evidence, now add one final comment:

I was disposed to be pleased [with Nature]. I am a lover of Nature and an admirer of Beauty. I can bear fatigue and welcome privation, and have seen some of the noblest views in the world. But in all this—the recollections of bitterness, and more especially of recent and more home desolation, which must accompany me through life, have preyed upon me here; and neither the music of the Shepherd, the crashing of the Avalanche, nor the torrent, the mountain, the Glacier, the Forest, nor the Cloud, have for one moment lightened the weight upon my heart, nor enabled me to lose my own wretched identity in the majesty, and the power, and the Glory, around, above, and beneath me.[12]

10. *L & J,* III, 359–360.
11. *L & J,* III, 369.
12. *L & J,* III, 364.

No evidence can be found in Byron's private correspondence to confirm any such feeling of mysticism or pantheistic deification of Nature as that suggested by a few passages in the poems of this period. On the contrary, the interest expressed in his letters seems to be that of an appreciative, slightly mischievous tourist with a realistic, scientific bent. Interpretation of those rare "mystical" moments in his verse must then be regulated by a recognition of Byron's real experiences among the Alps. He observed, he appreciated, and he felt; but he did not commune, and he did not "merge." In the poetry he wrote about responses to Nature which he wanted to feel, exaggerating the love for natural phenomena in order to convince himself that such affection was possible.

To assert that solitude is a central motif of *The Prisoner of Chillon, Childe Harold's Pilgrimage,* and *Manfred* adds little to the body of critical commentary on these poems; but to consider in connection with them a statement by Byron on the effects of isolation may provide new understanding of their themes, characterizations, and metaphorical devices. Solitude, Byron once observed,

has but one disadvantage . . . but that is a serious one—it is apt to give one too high an opinion of oneself. In the world we are sure to be reminded of every known or supposed defect we may have; hence we can rarely, unless possessed of an inordinate share of vanity, form a very exalted opinion of ourselves. . . . But, to return to solitude . . . it is the only fool's paradise on earth: there we have no one to remind us of our faults, or by whom we can be humiliated by comparisons. Our evil passions sleep, because they are not excited; our productions appear sublime, because we have no kind and judicious friend to hint at their defects, and to point out faults of style and imagery where we had thought ourselves most luminous: these are the advantages of solitude, and those who have once tasted them, can never return to the busy world again with any zest for its feverish enjoyments.[13]

Scarcely to the point here is the erroneous psychological assumption that "evil passions" somehow hibernate in isolation, or the autobiographical irony in the qualifying phrase about vanity, or the possible confession of the author's error in seeking to escape the outraged

13. *Conversations of Lord Byron with the Countess of Blessington* (London: R. Bentley, 1834), pp. 335–337.

cries of London bluestockings in 1816. What I wish to stress is Byron's possible evaluative glance at the motives of Childe Harold, Manfred, and most particularly, the Prisoner of Chillon. Each of these personae, whether as the result of personal choice or external pressure, exists in a world destitute of meaningful human contact; and each endeavors to construct imaginatively a "fool's paradise on earth" in which his defects of character are obscured, and the restraints of mortality are denied or transcended, through the exercise of an incremental egocentricism. All three protagonists strive to transform (or disfigure) the nature of reality according to the requirements of their injured, alienated beings in order to achieve a "very exalted opinion" of themselves. Largely successful in that effort, the Prisoner is destined to regain his freedom "with a sigh."

I

The Prisoner of Chillon[14] is not so much a story about "the restoration of the life urge"[15] as it is the narrative of a proud, garrulous, and self-indulgent old man who satisfies the demands of his ego by retelling, and vicariously reliving, a crisis in his history from which he never fully recovered.[16] With the validity and justification of three

14. Karl Kroeber remarks that "despair induced by isolation is possibly Byron's commonest motif in his early tales, but in *Chillon* he portrays the growth of that emotion meticulously and in detail. His descriptions become functional to his characterizations. . . . Not merely *what* happened but *how* it happened is increasingly his preoccupation" (*Romantic Narrative Art* [Madison: University of Wisconsin Press, 1960], p. 144). See also Andrew Rutherford (*Byron: A Critical Study* [Stanford: Stanford University Press, 1961]): "Byron [in *Chillon*] shows a hitherto unsuspected power of dramatic imagination—an ability to create and sustain a different type of character, to 'imitate' convincingly emotions and psychological states that he himself had not experienced" (p. 75).

15. William H. Marshall, *The Structure of Byron's Major Poems* (Philadelphia: University of Pennsylvania Press, 1962), p. 87.

16. The notion that the Prisoner is Bonnivard has been justly discredited by Marshall (pp. 82 and 183, note 3). It seems to me likely that Byron's note to the poem ("When this poem was composed, I was not sufficiently aware of the history of Bonnivard, as I should have endeavored to dignify the subject by an attempt to celebrate his courage and virtues") was occasioned by public identification of the Prisoner and Bonnivard. That Byron did not celebrate the "courage and virtues" of the protagonist, but something other, lends credibility, I think, to the following interpretation.

ethical-psychological attitudes he must impress himself and his audience: (1) that his conduct has been consistently exemplary; (2) that his philosophic negativism is the legitimate consequence of his captivity and the loss of his brothers; and (3) that he is a kind of super-hero for having survived at all the isolation of the dungeon. His neurotic introspection prevents the Prisoner from recognizing that his present failure to locate any cause for happiness evolves directly from his earlier failure to capitalize upon the opportunities for spiritual and emotional development offered by physical confinement and the self-sacrifice of others: given a chance to learn the meaning of freedom, he learns only "to love despair." The poem is to a limited degree about growth through suffering, spiritual insight induced by physical pain; it is chiefly about stunted growth, astigmatic vision, and abortive rebirth.

The dramatic monologue opens with the speaker's generalized recapitulation of the conditions which produced his "grey" hair, "bowed" limbs, and broken spirit. He has endured the privation of "goodly earth and air," "suffered chains and courted death," and witnessed the annihilation of his family "for my father's faith . . . For tenets he would not forsake." Thrice alluding to the father within thirteen lines, the speaker insists upon his loyalty to the "lineal race," and therefore calls attention emphatically to what he interprets as his own self-sacrificial defense of religious principles in which he held only vicarious stock. Beyond some familial pride in "Persecution's rage," he indicates no personal commitment to the parent's religious beliefs; the stress is consistently upon self-denial for his father's sake. As the last remaining "wreck" of his family, the narrator unconsciously transfers responsibility for his misery to his religious heritage, and simultaneously congratulates himself for sacrificing liberty in favor of devotion to family.

Reflection upon his father and five brothers now reminds the speaker of the "seven pillars of Gothic mould, / In Chillon's dungeons," which became for him during the imprisonment symbols of the family—"massy and grey," but firmly united in purpose to the last. The "greyness" or "dimness" of the columns (recalling the "grey" hair image and anticipating the metaphorical darkening of the dungeon) is partially relieved by a

> dull imprisoned ray,
> A sunbeam which hath lost its way,
> And through the crevice and the cleft
> Of the thick wall is fallen and left.
>
> (ll. 30–33)

From the commencement of their confinement, this is to say, the prisoners were granted a "ray" of encouragement, reassurance, from the external, free world; consumed with despair over their misfortune, they develop amaurosis and cannot perceive, or at least interpret correctly, their single source of relief. Correspondingly, as the speaker grows more intent upon depicting and re-experiencing the horrible loneliness of the dungeon, he steadily emphasizes blackness and blindness. This figure of sunlight penetrating cold and stony darkness, moreover, constitutes the first of several instances in the poem where images of life and death are fused: on the one hand we have sunlight and warmth, and on the other, stones, columns, iron chains, and gloom. The psychological tension of the narrator between repudiation of the dark chill of death and discovery of the meaning of the light is skillfully mirrored throughout by the juxtaposition of these opposing figures.

The speaker's death-wish, his pathological dependence upon former relationships, and his failure to reconcile previous restrictions with the opportunities of a "new day," are all obvious in lines 40–44.[17] Indeed, the sun (later explicitly linked with the youngest brother of the narrator) has not risen since "my last brother drooped and died, / And I lay living by his side." Hence, time too has ceased for the speaker: "I lost their [the years'] long and heavy score;" and preparation for what Marshall calls the "emotional climax" of the poem in stanza 9 is complete. Anguish induced by memory is the distinguishing feature of the speaker's static existence; by reconstructing and recounting the adversity of prison life, he attempts to alleviate his malaise and exonerate himself for failing to seize his several opportunities for regeneration.

The stress in stanzas 1 and 2 on visual imagery continues briefly in

17. These lines of course convincingly foreshadow the conclusion of the narrative. We know at this point that freedom means nothing to the narrator; we need to find out why.

the third stanza ("We could not see . . . But with that pale and livid light / That made us strangers") before shifting to auditory figures. Impercipient of the light, the brothers "hearken to each other's speech," recite some "legend old" or "song heroically bold" in search of consolation. But even as the opacity of the dungeon seems to transform their appearance, so their voices also "took a dreary tone, / An echo of the dungeon stone." Admitting that "It might be fancy," the Prisoner nevertheless claims that their speech "never sounded like our own." The confinement thus begins to exhaust and alter the brothers, and, apparently, gradually to strip them of individual identity; mere shadows of their former selves, they seem to die, in fact, to each other in their isolation ("we were three—yet, each alone").

But the speaker hastens to reinvest each of the brothers and himself with their former individuality, as though still unwilling squarely to confront the disaster wrought by their imprisonment. None too modestly, he confesses that as "the eldest of the three," he should have strengthened and cheered the others, and that he did so; "And each did well in his degree." Now recognition of the responsibilities of an eldest brother is quite a different thing from priding oneself on surviving what others of less degree could not resist. By complimenting himself here on the sustenance he offered his brothers, the speaker reveals a kind of self-indulgent vanity on withstanding better than all the afflictions of incarceration. Predictably, then, he shifts to an analysis of the anxiety of his own mind induced by the anguish of his youngest brother, that kinsman "with eyes as blue as heaven":

> truly might it [my soul] be distressed
> To see such bird in such a nest;
> For he was beautiful as day—
>   (When day was beautiful to me
>   As to young eagles, being free)—
>   A polar day, which will not see
> A sunset till its summer's gone,
>   Its sleepless summer of long light,
> The snow-clad offspring of the sun:
>   And thus he was as pure and bright.
>   (ll. 77–86)

The figurative association of the youngest brother with light and freely-soaring birds explicitly anticipates, of course, the later visita-

tion of the bird to the dungeon window and the momentary gleam of
light it brings to mitigate the narrator's gloom. But equally, and
ironically, implicit in these lines is the speaker's failure to recognize
that his release, without stipulation of any sort, has provided him
with the sort of liberty and "long light" reflected in the countenance
of the youngest brother. The juxtaposition of the brother's zest and
liveliness with the speaker's ennui and bondage to memory intensifies
the irony of his failure to learn from experience.

If, as I think, the youngest brother may be considered a symbolic
representation of innocent, irresponsible, passive freedom, the middle
brother should be interpreted as an embodiment of the active, defiant, combative spirit of liberty—unfit "in chains to pine". (We need
not see these symbolic values as consciously imposed by the speaker
upon the characters; his response to recollection of his brothers suggests that the symbolic equation has been registered unconsciously.)
The middle brother was

> formed to combat with his kind;
> Strong in his frame, and of a mood
> Which 'gainst the world in war had stood,
> And perished in the foremost rank
> With joy . . . .
>   (ll. 93–97)

A "hunter of the hills," a pursuer of deer and wolf, he is by nature
incapable of subsisting in confinement; "His spirit withered" in
chains. Now the significant point here is that each brother illustrates
one component of the narrator's character, and each is eventually
influential in motivating him to an emotional and a physical response. On the one hand the innocent yearning for freedom without
responsibility is imaged in the speaker's response to the visitation of
the bird; and on the other hand, the need for responsible, active, self-
assistance is figured in his efforts to carve a footing in the wall of the
dungeon. The magnetism of the two brothers is both inhibiting (insofar as the narrator's memory is concerned) and liberating (insofar as
it prompts him to action), but he ultimately fails to fuse, or even
recognize, the two complementary forces after his release.

Life and death are again forcefully merged in the image of the
dungeon set deep within the "massy waters" of Lake Leman, a thousand feet from "Chillon's snow-white battlement": "A double dun-

geon wall and wave / Have made—and like a living grave." The
auditory images of stanza 3 are now reintroduced and joined by
tactual figures:

> We heard it [Lake Leman] ripple night and day;
>   Sounding o'er our heads it knocked;
> And I have felt the winter's spray
> Wash through the bars when winds were high
> And wanton in the happy sky;
>   And then the very rock hath rocked,
>   And I have felt it shake, unshocked,
> Because I could have smiled to see
> The death that would have set me free.
>   (ll. 117–125)

Metaphorically allied with wild wind and a "happy sky," water, like
the "dull, imprisoned ray," is not a sadistic reminder of the liberty
denied the prisoners, but rather is a source of potential encouragement, a hint that life goes on without, and should within, the confines
of the walls. Stubbornly oblivious to the meaning of the water, the
speaker feels it shake the rock without comprehending the necessity
of adjusting his desires for physical release to the possibilities for
spiritual liberty. The "message" of the light and water, and later of
the bird, is that intellectual or spiritual freedom can be preserved
and deepened even under the most difficult physical circumstances.
Ironically, the narrator (ll. 124–125) makes no distinction between
physical and spiritual liberty; he prefers death to either.

The allusions to "cold earth" and "turfless earth" in stanza 7
paradoxically anticipate the warm floral and light figures of stanza 8.
The youngest brother is here described as "the flower . . . who
withered on the stalk away;" "He faded . . . So softly worn, so
sweetly weak;" he was marked by a

>   cheek whose bloom
> Was as a mockery of the tomb,
> Whose tints as gently sunk away
> As a departing rainbow's ray;
> An eye of most transparent light,
> That almost made the dungeon bright.
>   (ll. 190–195)

In his retelling, the narrator lingers longingly over the details of his brother's death (stressing his kinship with light), over his own agony at being abandoned, over his near hysteria in recognizing the breakage of that "dearest link" which "bound me to my failing race." Then, in what is possibly the most effective paradox of the poem, the severance of that "dearest link" from life momentarily endows the speaker with the strength to break his material chains at the instant when physical liberty means least to him. Thus free, however, he finds himself in more profound despair: the dungeon becomes "this black spot;" his own hand is "full as chill" as his brother's; and he is wracked with a "frantic feeling" of loss and futility.

Physical and emotional paralysis in stanza 9[18] reduce the narrator to a mere brute, more dead than alive, almost indistinguishable from the stones around him. The nadir of his experience is imagistically distilled in the dissipation of all objective realities by which he might orient and hence identify himself. Conscious only of a deadening weightiness, a stultifying thickness in the prison, he collapses in severe shock. With the death of the youngest brother, therefore, not only does light vanish, but spatial and temporal perception as well.

But the regenerative process begins in stanza 10 with the synaesthetic image of "light" in the form of a bird's "carol" which "broke" in upon the "brain" of the narrator. The fusion of the images is perfectly appropriate, first, to the complete collapse of sensory perception represented in the previous stanza, and second, to the natural confusion of the senses upon being suddenly reactivated. Similarly, the speaker's physical and emotional responses to the presence of the bird are indeterminate and inconsistent: the carol is the "sweetest song ear ever heard" and his eyes "Ran over with the glad surprise" until his senses returned to their "wonted track." The visitation of the bird has been in one respect singularly effective: the Prisoner's senses are revitalized. He sees once more not only the "dungeon walls and floor," but also the "glimmer of the sun," the "azure wings" of the bird, and he hears the "song that said a thousand things." At the same time that the bird revives "feeling," however, it reawakens "thought"; and with thought comes the narrator's con-

---

18. See Marshall's excellent interpretation of this stanza, pp. 91–92.

scious effort to identify himself with the bird, and thence the bird with the soul of his brother—at which point the bird proves its mortality by flying away: "For he would never thus have flown— / And left me twice so doubly lone." The central issue here is, I think, that the narrator, like so many other protagonists in Byron's canon, has failed properly to integrate thought with feeling, to modify the one with the other, to merge his sensory with his intellectual responses to the bird's song. The function of the bird surely is to reawaken the speaker to the continuity of life (and hence, in terms of the poem's imagery, to light) in the outside world; but the speaker can only describe his condition after the bird's departure as a dark blot in an otherwise brilliantly illuminated universe. He is

> Lone—as a solitary cloud,
>   A single cloud on a sunny day,
> When all the rest of heaven is clear,
> A frown upon the atmosphere,
> That hath no business to appear
>   When skies are blue and earth is gay.
>   (ll. 294–299)

I have suggested the possibility of interpreting the younger brother as a symbolic representation of innocent, wanton, youthful freedom. That brother's repeated association with light, birds, and color, and the recurrence of those same motifs in stanza 10, make it clear that the younger kinsman's freedom is the sort offered to the speaker here. He rejects it by his concentration upon the death of his brother and his own consequent loneliness.

Gradually, however, the influence of the middle brother takes over and bestirs the narrator into physical activity. He is now at liberty to move about the dungeon, to stroll from "side to side," "athwart," and "round the pillars one by one." Eventually (stanza 12), he makes "a footing in the wall," not, he assures us, to escape, but because

> I was curious to ascend
> To my barred windows, and to bend
> Once more, upon the mountains high,
> The quiet of a loving eye.
>   (ll. 328–331)

If we remember that the middle brother has twice (ll. 103 and 143) been associated with mountains, and that he represents assertive, combative, responsible freedom, we may suspend indictment of the speaker in the hope that he will yet find encouragement and *raison d'être* in a view of the countryside—a view of which the bird and its song were prescient symbols. The fact of the matter is, however, that the narrator's response is a foregone conclusion; he has already made up his mind *not* to recognize the productive picture of life before him: "the whole earth would henceforth be / A wider prison unto me." His motive, therefore, seems to be a masochistic desire to augment awareness of his isolation and confinement by observing a world of communication and liberty.

What the narrator does see is a kaleidoscopic panorama of vigorous life in its richest forms: the "Rhone in fullest flow," the "leap and gush" of torrents, the "white-walled distant town," the "whiter sails," the "small green isle" with "three tall trees," the "young flowers growing," the "joyous" fish, and, finally, the eagle riding the "rising blast." With the sight of the eagle his mind reverts to the youngest brother:

> And then new tears came in my eye,
> And I felt troubled—and would fain
> I had not left my recent chain;
> And when I did descend again,
> The darkness of my dim abode
> Fell on me as a heavy load;
> It was as is a new-dug grave,
> Closing o'er one we sought to save,—
> And yet my glance, too much opprest,
> Had almost need of such a rest.
>   (ll. 356–365)

This is a disappointing but not unexpected response. The narrator has not the remotest intention of releasing himself from the bondage of memory; his reasoning of the last two lines above is pure rationalization, for not until he beheld the eagle had he found the view exhausting. Notice, too, that the dungeon assumes its old appearance of darkness, or dimness, and that the smell of death hangs thickly about the cell. The speaker abandons himself to utter despair.

The final stanza offers nothing but more proof that any kind of affirmation about the continuity of life or the meaning of liberty is now impossible for the speaker. When his physical bonds are cast off, he finds himself a slave to emotional retrospection: "I learned to love despair." He has constructed for himself a "fool's paradise," a hermitage whose foundation is a self-pitying, self-indulgent dependence on the past. That he has made friends with spiders and mice is only another indication of his separation from and incapacity for human relationships. Isolated so long from human intercourse, he prefers to avoid it entirely: the tale itself is an attempt to justify his unfitness for communal existence. It is ultimately his failure to recognize and capitalize upon the opportunities for spiritual growth offered by physical incarceration that leads him to lament, "I / Regained my freedom with a sigh."

II

Most critical efforts to discover a structural or thematic unity in the Third Canto of *Childe Harold's Pilgrimage*[19] have proved unsuccessful because they proceed on the erroneous notion that the narrator is a static figure: i.e., that he manifests no appreciable change during or at the end of his narrative, that he emerges at the conclusion unschooled by his experiences, ignorant of any value they may have held for him. Scholars in general maintain that Harold[20] still suffers from emotional stagnation, spiritual emptiness, and psychological instability, that his self-torturing introversion still excludes him from any meaningful human contact, and that he consequently must wander on, isolated, alienated, bitterly disenchanted with himself and his world.

---

19. Of these, Marshall's complex analysis (pp. 72–81) is the most persuasive.

20. All biographical correlations aside, the poem may be regarded as a dramatic monologue in which the speaker and the protagonist are identifiable. Attempts to distinguish between the two have created more complexities than they have solved; hence, to my mind, it seems more useful to interpret the character of Harold himself as a fictive embodiment of the narrator's restlessness and grief and suffering. Considered in this manner, the poem achieves a much tighter cohesiveness and a clearly discernible structural and thematic unity. The terms "Harold," "narrator," and "speaker" are therefore used interchangeably in the following discussion.

This in fact is not the case at all. Ample evidence warrants consideration of the poem as the speaker's conscious and partially successful search for spiritual equilibrium, his quest for emotional regeneration or a revitalization of his affective responses, which would culminate in a perception of the merit of human fellowship on either a physical or spiritual plane. The antithetical tendencies of Harold's thought practically convulse his emotional framework: on the one hand, his conscious determination to prolong isolation because of his conviction that exposure to humanity can lead only to increased disillusionment over man's grievous condition; and on the other hand, his equally strong though unconscious belief—registered in the vigor of his rationalizations, the exaggeration of his rhetoric, and the violence of his attempts to identify himself with Nature[21]—that continued solitude promises him only deeper despair and intensified anguish because it provides no objective standard of thought and conduct by which his temperamental extravagances can be judged, ordered, and regulated. The speaker, therefore, fluctuates between his emotional desire to indulge and cultivate his *Weltschmerz* by refusing any antidote for it, and his intellectual awareness of the need to develop human relationships as the most congenial method of achieving a stable, satisfying maturity. Once again, the incompatibility of flesh and spirit, body and soul, is the fundamental issue:[22] Harold's repeatedly frustrated efforts to project his own ego into objects of natural or historical interest eventually force him to recognize the claims of the body and the possibilities for relief offered by the cultivation of human love. In other words, at the last he aban-

21. *"Childe Harold* is a series of . . . symbolic projections of the ego into the external world, reshaping and redefining it in terms of itself. . . . The bleaker his vision of man's fate, the more desperate is Byron's effort to make himself felt and noticed; he will somehow force even the mindless universe to pay attention to him" (Edward E. Bostetter, *The Romantic Ventriloquists* [Seattle: University of Washington Press, 1963], p. 268).

22. "Byron's romantic desire . . . is frustrated not only by external reality but by inward division. On the one hand his egotism . . . constantly bursts through its rationalizing garments of benevolism, pantheism, transcendentalism, and evolutionary idealism, and betrays itself in stark nakedness. On the other hand his ego was not a concentrated drive but a ferment of conflicts" (H. N. Fairchild, *Religious Trends in English Poetry,* 5 vols. [New York: Columbia University Press, 1939–1957], III, 413).

dons his futile efforts to become absorbed into the abstract principle Love, and, instead, learns to derive a degree of satisfaction and hope from the undeniable affections of his heart.

Almost all commentators have noted Byron's attempt to envelop the poem in addresses to his daughter, Ada. But none has explored the dramatic potentialities of the daughter-figure; none has noted the organic relationship of the two apostrophes to the rest of the poem; and none has discussed in any detail the alteration of tone and emphasis in the concluding statement. The daughter, I think, functions dramatically and organically as the force which ultimately compels the narrator to perceive and admit the danger of isolation from human relationships. Moreover, the "image" of the daughter, recurring at strategic points throughout the poem, and its effect upon the speaker, should be contrasted with the "images" of various historical figures (Napoleon, Rousseau, etc.), with the frequent nature images, and the effect of all these upon Harold. Initially, the narrator recoils from physical contact with all humanity—he can attempt empathic identification with historical characters and with Nature without risking, as he thinks, defilement by the masses. But gradually the intensity of his agony in failing to accomplish successfully the identification constrains him to recognize the desirability of "loving" his daughter, compels him, that is, to substitute a specific and concrete love for the general and abstract "Love" with which he has sought to link himself.

Furthermore, within this larger framework, the structure of the Third Canto may be described as a series of emotional oscillations between the extremes of abysmal, self-indulgent despair and lofty, idealistic hope: Harold no sooner rises imaginatively to the mountain-peaks than he collapses wretchedly back into the valley of despondency, only to rise again because he can do nothing else. Byron's emphasis, however, is steadily upon the decreasing distance between the two extremities, and the last four stanzas, although comprising no reconciliation, do represent an emotional leveling-off, a relaxation of the tensions, an abatement of the pressures which have agitated the speaker throughout. Harold's vacillation between these opposing planes of existence is communicated primarily through a dialectical pattern of imagery in the poem: on the one hand, for example, are figures of cloud-piercing birds, towering summits, scintillating lightnings, dynamic natural life, and impetuous animation; on the other hand are figures of destructive vultures, gloomy caverns, cataclysmic battles, decaying castles, sterile and rotting natural objects. Recurring almost cyclically, the images serve as barometric gauges of Harold's emotional condition. The speaker does not always *tell* the truth; but what he sees and what he chooses to record are reliable guides at any given moment to his actual state of mind.

The opening address to Ada associates her with the "fair face" of her mother, characterizes her as the "sole daughter of my house and heart," and recalls that the former parting of father and offspring, unlike the present one, was "with a hope." Whatever biographical significance these lines may contain, the essential point is that they paradoxically foreshadow the "hopefulness," the qualified note of optimism, on which the poem closes. No cheerful confidence that father and daughter will be physically reunited informs the conclusion; but a firm belief that the two are joined in spirit, that the speaker, at last successfully outside himself, is "wrapt" in love for his child, indicates material progress on his part toward psychological adjustment. At any rate, the themes of isolation and despair, occasioned to some degree by the separation of parent and daughter, are forcefully launched in the first five lines, and we are prepared for the narrator's lengthy lucubration on his misery.

The distinguishing characteristics of the speaker are physical passivity and emotional sterility; in a word, an unresponsiveness to external stimuli of any sort. Equally oblivious to water and wind, he admits that nothing could "grieve or glad mine eye;" his voyage is not a matter of choice, for he is victimized by forces beyond his control:

> I am as a *weed,*
> *Flung* from the rock, on Ocean's foam, to sail
> Where'er the *surge* may sweep, the *tempest's breath* prevail.[23]
>
> (st. ii)

23. Unless otherwise specified, the italics throughout this discussion of *Childe Harold* are my own and are used to indicate recurring imagistic motifs, or repeated configurations of one sort or another, which figure forth the warring elements of Harold's mind or simply his spiritual plight.

With neither purpose nor direction to guide his pilgrimage, he again determines to sing about "the wandering outlaw of his own dark mind"—the same theme which occupied his "youth's summer." He will recklessly "bear it with me, as the *rushing wind* / Bears the cloud onwards," for in that theme he finds

> The furrows of long thought, and dried-up tears,
> Which, ebbing, leave a *sterile track* behind,
> O'er which all heavily the journeying years
> Plod the last *sands of life,*—where *not a flower appears.*
>
> (st. iii)

These passages merit detailed examination, for despite the confusion of the images (How, for example, can dried-up tears ebb?) they present figuratively the narrator's condition: the images of the up-rooted weed, of summertime, of unproductive furrows, of dried-up tears, of the sterile track, of sand, and of absent vegetation summarily demonstrate *at this moment* Harold's emotional and intellectual sterility. He no longer retains the capacity to experience passion spontaneously (st. iv), and he recognizes the probable futility of attempting to sing at all: his purpose is merely to "fling / Forgetfulness" around himself. Having pierced the depths of life, he is incapacitated to feel "Love, Sorrow, Fame, Ambition, Strife" (cf. st. cxi), and his thought seeks refuge in

> lone caves, yet rife
> With airy images, and shapes which dwell
> Still unimpaired, though old, in the Soul's haunted cell.
>
> (st. v)

Now the ironic upshot of these lines, in contrast to stanzas ii and iii, is that Harold has protested too much: he is not in fact as immune to emotional stimuli as he would have us believe. He has clearly preserved some affective faculty or he could not so energetically respond to despair, nor could he perceive the "airy images" in the cave to which his thought retreats. The retention of "airy images, and shapes" (symbols of Harold's ideal aspirations) in the speaker's thought is reliable evidence that the struggle between emotion and intellect continues. Harold wishes to convince himself that feelings of any sort precipitate disaster, but he is demonstrably incapable of escaping their influence. His rationalizations here merely betray his real plight.

In an active repudiation of the earlier sterility configurations, Harold now vows (st. vi) to "create" and live more "intensely" by endowing "fancy" with "form." His resolution represents the first of several examples in the poem of an affirmative "therapeutic aesthetic idealism,"[24] for he attempts to objectify, and hence render manageable, the warring elements of his own mind, thereby providing a release for tensions and a contingency for reconciliation. But Harold does not transcend the limitations of his own being, as Bloom maintains, nor does he totally blend himself with the birth of what he creates. The pairing of form and fancy strongly suggests the familiar body-soul, flesh-spirit dichotomy, and the speaker immediately draws a distinction between the "nothingness" of the body and the congenial substantiality of the "Soul of my thought." Another of Byron's equivalents for the Romantic Imagination, this "soul" replenishes his diminishing supply of "feelings" and stimulates his creative impulses. But it is at once a blessing and a curse: the aspiring imagination cannot accommodate itself to a "clay" body, and even in the process of creating, Harold is steadily conscious of the disparity between what he is and what he should be, of the fixed gulf, that is, between the world of the senses and the world of the imagination. "Mixed" and "blended" with the spirit (or "soul") of his thought, his imaginative awareness is a source of joy and pain.

His reluctance to "feel," therefore, is based upon his knowledge of the psychological frenzy to which feeling can lead unless disciplined by an intellectual perception of the limitations of mortality. The brain can become *"boiling"* and "o'erwrought" in its own *"eddy," "A whirling gulf of phantasy and flame;" "Fire"* vanishes from the mind, as "vigour from the limb;" "Life's enchanted cup but *sparkles* near the brim;" the *"springs* of life" become *"poisoned;"* one must *"feed on bitter fruits"* and "dregs" of "wormwood." The penalty for attempting to deny the existence of that invisible, fettering *"chain"* of mortality which "galled for ever" is severe indeed, but Harold, "of

24. Harold Bloom, *The Visionary Company* (New York: Doubleday and Company, 1961), p. 234.

the breast which fain no more would feel," is incapable of submitting to the restrictions of that chain. Though "Secure in guarded *coldness*" and "*sheathed* with an invulnerable mind," his heart still responds, though bitterly and negatively, to external stimuli:

> But who can view the ripened rose, nor seek
>   To wear it? who can curiously behold
> The smoothness and the sheen of Beauty's cheek,
> Nor feel the heart can never all grow old?
> Who can contemplate Fame through clouds unfold
> The *star* which rises o'er her steep, nor climb?
>
> (st. xi)

A detached, objective perspective is impossible for Harold: the need to feel and the urge to climb are his most compelling drives. So again he plunges *"within the vortex"* and rolls "On with the *giddy circle*" (cf. st. vii): unable to accept the alternatives open to him, despairing of reconciliation, and having no determinate goal, Harold passively surrenders himself to the whims of wind and wave.

As the "most unfit / Of men to herd with Man" because he cannot "yield dominion of his mind," Harold proposes to find a "life within itself," and promptly admits his inability to do so by turning to striking natural phenomena which seem to speak a "mutual language." His efforts to identify himself with mountains, oceans, breakers, and their like instantly prove futile; observation of the stars only causes him to populate "them with beings bright / As their own beams" (cf. the form-fancy idea)—that is, anthropomorphically, with beings like Harold's idealized version of himself. The brief and unsatisfactory projection of the ego into the stars only aggravates awareness of his dreary condition:

> Could he have kept his spirit to that flight
> He had been happy; but this *clay* will *sink*
> Its *spark* immortal, envying it the *light*
> To which it *mounts,* as if to break the *link*
> That keeps us from yon heaven which woos us to its brink.
>
> (st. xiv)

The jealous clay, this is to say, becomes an imprisoning cage, and the aspiring soul, like a *"wild-born falcon with clipt wing"* which beats

"His breast and beak against his wiry dome," is so seared with heat that it *"eats"* through the narrator's bosom. The figures of the wild enkindled spirit and the cold fettering clay represent, of course, the dual opposites of Harold's character which he seeks throughout the poem to harmonize. Presently unable to accomplish the reconciliation, he in effect pampers his despair by finding in it a "smilingness;" and, like *"wild"* mariners on a faltering ship who "madly" dose themselves with "intemperate" draughts, he permits the knowledge of the vanity of human endeavor to anesthetize the emotion which would now deny the fact. By an irrational revelry in melancholy, he finds "cheer."

At the nadir of dejection, Harold abruptly shakes himself loose of it by describing the battlefield of Waterloo (st. xvii–xx). All of his egocentric posturing and sentimental attitudinizing vanish for the moment, and he engages in clear, objective, historical analysis. He has not, however, entirely escaped the galling sense of himself, for an unconscious and paradoxical awareness of his own slavery to mortality vitiates all of his reflections upon liberty. But he does exhibit a temporary self-forgetfulness in his speculations upon the universal effect of Wellington's victory.

Harold is forcibly struck, first of all, by the absence of some "colossal bust" or "column" to mark the "place of skulls," this "grave of France;"[25] and, second, by the distinctive and ironic contrast between the destruction wrought by the battle and the present vegetation of the field, as though the site had been fertilized by the "red rain" of blood. Generalizing from these two issues, he reflects upon the transience of fame and the impermanence of all things in an image of the *"eagle"* (cf. st. xv) which flew in " 'pride of place' " before being "Pierced by the shaft of banded nations." All of Napoleon's ambition and labors, all of the suffering and endurance of European nations, Harold speculates, are for nothing if liberty has not been permanently achieved: "Shall we, who struck the Lion down . . . Pay the Wolf homage?" The only goal worth the strife is

25. "The scenery and monuments which evoke the ravages of time and the ruin of men's aspirations are not merely illustrative of *sic transit gloria mundi*. They are, rather, symbols of the contemporary spiritual condition" (Kroeber, pp. 138–139), or, at least, of Harold's condition.

unqualified freedom—"when the myrtle wreathes a Sword." The general intent of these lines, though doubtless an unconscious one, is that all hardship and privation profit nothing unless some *positive* goal is attained: mere suffering and endurance for their own sakes are meaningless. And perhaps Harold vaguely senses the applicability of his conclusions to himself and his situation.

Harold's imaginative re-creation of the Duchess of Richmond's ball and the ensuing battle (sts. xxi–xxviii), organically integrated with the themes of the poem, represents another of the speaker's efforts to project himself, and hence lose his identity, in the brisk activity of the celebration and the military engagement. Aside from the splendid (and obvious) use of imagistic contrast through the account, two other points of interest emerge: the delay of the dancers in awakening to the imminence of disaster; and their speed and impetuosity in meeting their responsibilities once they understand them. In their almost primitive savagery—their "fierce native daring"—all sense of self-protection is blurred by their absorption in military action. Harold himself is of course unreasonably slow to see the personal disaster consequent upon the continuation of his self-pitying reflections, and he needs desperately to merge himself in some spectacular activity in which self-awareness will be obliterated. Imaginative re-creation of the battle is one means to that end.

But it is only temporarily effective. Harold is gradually overcome first by a sense of the futility of human effort, and second by a sense of his own imprisoned and thwarted aspirations. The "unreturning brave," he prophesies, in a figure recalling the imagistic contrast of stanza xvii, will before evening

> be trodden like the grass
> Which now beneath them, but above shall grow
> In its next verdure, when this *fiery* mass
> Of living Valour, rolling on the foe
> And *burning with high Hope,* shall *moulder cold and low.*
>
> (st. xxvii)

Such figures cannot but remind Harold of his earlier self-characterization in similar terms. But for the moment he singles out Howard of Carlisle for special praise.

The descriptive process to this point has been from an initial concentration upon Napoleon to an expansion outward to include the entire host of warriors; now we focus downward on the single hero and, thence, inward upon Harold himself. Though ostensibly contrasting Spring renewal with the dead veterans of Waterloo, Harold actually describes his own failure to find hope or even relevance to himself in the natural resuscitation. Hence, he emphasizes the "ghastly gap" in the lives of relatives who lost loved ones in the battle, particularly stressing his own sluggishness resulting from the *"fever of vain longing."* In an extended series of metaphors (st. xxxii–xxxiii), more apropos of Harold than of the kinsmen he proposes to discuss, the speaker anatomizes the pain of living with a broken heart. He has indeed moved rather far now from Waterloo and here is immersed in a consciousness of personal discontent and loneliness. In each of the metaphors the contrast between appearance and reality, between external life or continuity and internal death or decay, is explicit:

> The *tree will wither* long before it fall;
> The *hull drives on,* though mast and sail be torn;
> The roof-tree sinks, but *moulders* on the hall
> In massy hoariness; the ruined wall
> Stands when its wind-worn battlements are gone;
> The bars survive the captive they enthrall;
> The day drags through though storms keep out the sun.
>
> (st. xxxii)

Or, he continues, the broken heart will live on "Even as a broken Mirror, which the glass / In every fragment multiplies." The significant point here is that despite all of Harold's protests to the contrary, the "heart" which will not "forsake" does live on, in "shattered guise;" though he describes his heart as "still" and "cold" and "bloodless," it is impossible to believe him because that same heart "aches" with "sleepless sorrow." His remarks here are simply a revised version of his admissions in stanza xi: this is all merely another exercise in self-deception. Harold still wishes to deny the claims of emotion, wishes to think himself spiritually dead, but he suffers with passionate intensity.

Recalling the "smilingness in Despair" figure, and reintroducing the image of the withering tree, Harold continues,

> There is a very life in our despair,
> *Vitality of poison,—a quick root*
> *Which feeds these deadly branches* . . . .
>
> (st. xxxiv)

The element of sorrow in life makes existence like "the *apples on the Dead Sea's shore,/* All *ashes to the taste*" (cf. stanza vii). Harold, then, has come full circle: he remains infatuated with his own grief but is unwilling to rid himself of it because it alone keeps him emotionally alive.

In a gradual swing away from this depth of self-recriminating despair, Harold now turns again to Napoleon, certainly with the initial purpose of identifying himself with the conqueror, but eventually moving to another detached evaluation of his character. Napoleon's spirit, he observes, was *"antithetically mixed"* (cf. st. vi), tending, as the moment dictated, toward either sublimity or triviality, but consistently toward extremity "in all things." Correspondingly, these stanzas on Napoleon all begin with, and are organized around, antitheses: the hero is "the greatest, nor the worst of men," the "Conqueror and Captive of the Earth," and either "more or less than man." Had he been of a moderate or compromising nature, he should never have gained his "throne;" for "Daring made thy *rise* as *fall*." Not only does Harold question the justice of Napoleon's conquests; he ironically contrasts the time when Fame was the Frenchman's wooer, his "Vassal," and the "flatterer" of his "fierceness," with the time when Napoleon himself became a slave first to Fame, then to his own "divinity." Although expert in "battling," commanding, and crushing, Napoleon is now reduced to a station below that of his "meanest soldier," because of his failure to govern his own "pettiest passion." Skilled in the psychology of his troops, he had no disposition for self-examination, and could not "learn that tempted Fate will leave *the loftiest Star*." The antitheses in these lines pit Napoleon's untamed emotional lust for power against his intellectual comprehension, overridden and negated by passion, of human character. Precisely like Harold in this respect, he could not see beyond himself long enough to see within himself.[26]

But that "untaught innate philosophy" (whether "Wisdom, Coldness, or deep Pride") had permitted Napoleon to withstand the turning tide of fortune. In the face of overwhelming adversity he had "smiled" with a "sedate and all-enduring eye," had, in fact, "stood unbowed" (cf. st. xvi). Although he had quite properly felt "scorn" for men and their thoughts, he had too frequently worn that despite on his "lip and brow," hence spurning the instruments that eventually precipitated his overthrow: his habitual aloofness and haughty cynicism turned men against him. It is, after all, this Napoleonic strength and Promethean endurance that Harold has consistently admired and that he clearly wishes to imitate. His identification with Napoleon in this respect is certain. But at the same time, he knows very well that he, also, has too much scorned the world and that his repudiation of humanity has in fact rendered him unfit to herd with men. Harold is nearly talking about himself again: his analysis of Napoleon is a shrewd and penetrating—though unconscious—examination of his own character.

Along the same lines Harold suggests furthermore that if Napoleon (and, by the process of the speaker's projection, himself) had been "like a *tower upon a headlong rock*"—that is, impervious to emotion, passion, the admiration or the scorn of men—he could have stood or fallen without mankind. But in another specific allusion to his own former and present emotional state of mind, Harold draws a revealing parallel between the cause of his own and Napoleon's inability to adjust themselves to isolation:

> But Quiet to quick bosoms is a Hell,
>   And *there*[27] hath been thy bane; there is a *fire*

26. See *PW*, II, 239, note 1: "In these stanzas . . . [Byron] bears witness to [Napoleon's] essential greatness, and, with manifest reference to his own personality and career, attributes his final downfall to the peculiar constitution of his genius and temper. . . . [Byron] could not fail to see, with insight quickened by self-knowledge, that greatness and genius possess no charm against littleness and commonness. "

27. Byron's emphasis.

> *And motion of the Soul which will not dwell*
> *In its own narrow being, but aspire*
> *Beyond the fitting medium of desire;*
> And, but once *kindled, quenchless* evermore,
> *Preys upon high adventure,* nor can tire
> Of aught but rest; *a fever at the core,*
> Fatal to him who bears, to all who ever bore.
>
> (st. xlii)

Still speaking in the third person, Harold on the one hand of course describes his own burning, feverish soul, his aspirations "beyond the fitting medium," and the fatality generated by his own heated bosom; but, on the other hand, he unconsciously seeks justification for his wretchedness by revealing the identical irreconcilables in characters of universal stature.

His self-indulgent introspection, then, is expectedly externalized and generalized (a recurring pattern in the poem): he refers to all "Conquerors and Kings," "Founders of sects and systems," "Sophists, Bards, Statesmen,"

> all *unquiet things*
> Which *stir* too strongly the *soul's secret springs,*
> And are themselves the fools to those they fool.
>   . . . what *stings*
> Are theirs! One breast laid open were a school
> Which would unteach mankind the *lust to shine or rule:*
> Their *breath is agitation,* and their life
> A *storm whereon they ride, to sink* at last.
>
> (sts. xlii–xliv)

In addition to further self-characterization here, Harold makes one important confession: if he is identifiable with all "unquiet things," then he is himself the fool of those he seeks to deceive. The observation is of course a cynical exaggeration, but the passage points again to the futility of capitulating to the demands of the feverish bosom and the impossibility of refraining from doing so. To deny the impulse of a "stinging breast" is to become as

> a *flame unfed,* which runs to *waste*
> With its own flickering, or *a sword laid by,*
> *Which eats into itself,* and rusts ingloriously.
>
> (st. xliv)

Similarly, the man who *ascends* will find himself on a chilly intermediary plateau between the warmth of heaven above and the "hating" community of mankind below. By surpassing or subduing mankind, one unfits himself to enjoy the "glow" of the "Sun of Glory" *or* the "spread" of "Earth and Ocean"—commits himself, that is, to endure *"icy rocks"* and *"Contending tempests"* without gaining anything in the process, since the *"loftiest peaks"* of Knowledge and Achievement are invariably "wrapt" in impenetrable "clouds and snow." The quest for fame or fortune or infinite knowledge or whatever may lead man to repudiate human ties, therefore, is doomed to terminate in an icy deadness of spirit, a cold and stagnant spiritual emptiness, far removed from the productive warmth of "Earth and Ocean."

The opposition of these sterile and dynamic figures immediately causes the narrator to shrink from the conclusion to which it obviously leads. Wearied of futile attempts to rationalize his own conduct by paralleling it with Napoleon's, and forced to recognize the disadvantageous condition to which unlimited aspiration commits him, Harold now tries almost hysterically to project himself into the natural splendor on the banks of the Rhine: he discovers there

> A blending of all beauties; streams and dells,
> Fruit, foliage, crag, wood, cornfield, mountain, vine,
> And *chiefless castles* breathing stern farewells
> From gray but leafy walls, where Ruin greenly dwells.
> (st. xlvi)

Now the significance of these lines lies not so much in Harold's perception of the harmony and unity of Nature—his perception is only momentary—but in his recognition of Nature's inability to transform "dead" objects into items of animation and growth which would conform to the remainder of the scene. In an image expressly recalling the earlier figures of the Dead Sea apples, the withered tree, and the others of stanza xxxii, Harold points to the vacant castle with gray walls where "Ruin greenly dwells." The progress of Nature has only concealed the corrupting influences of man by ornamenting the empty shell of a castle with evidence of life and activity. Thus, Harold ironically comments upon Nature's failure to alter what man has wrought and, inferentially, upon his immunity to her regenerative blessings. Among all the natural exhibits of dynamic organicism, Harold settles upon the rotting castle as a symbol of his spiritual dearth. The image is an important one, however, for its paradoxical opposite in stanzas xcix–ciii represents a certain measure of Harold's spiritual progress.

After a brief meditation upon man's reckless destruction of natural beauty, Harold apostrophizes the Rhine, stressing not the restorative powers of the river, but rather its ineffectiveness in erasing from his memory all former experiences: "o'er the blacken'd memory's blighting dream / Thy waves would vainly roll." Harold nearly slips back into torturous egomania here, but saves himself by admitting his sensibility to the loveliness of his environment. Though marked with "graven lines austere" and a "tranquil sternness, which had ta'en the place / Of *feelings fierier far* but less severe," Harold can now disclose that "Joy" is not entirely lost to him; its presence is only transient, but at least he admits his vulnerability to the effects of natural beauty.

The next three stanzas (liii–lv), occurring almost exactly midway in the poem, are crucial. Harold confesses, not quite truthfully, that his "days / Of Passion had *consumed themselves to dust,*" but claims, in an unexpected turnabout, that his capacity for love has not been completely sterilized:

> he felt,
> For there was soft Remembrance, and sweet Trust,
> In one fond breast, to which his own would melt,
> And in its tenderer hour on that his bosom dwelt.
>
> And he had learned to love . . .
> The helpless looks of *blooming Infancy,*
> Even in its earliest nurture . . .
> . . . though in solitude
> Small power the nipped affections have to grow,
> In him this *glowed* when all beside had *ceased to glow.*
>
> (sts. liii–liv)

The passage is important for several reasons. ructurally, it supplies a mid-point link between the mother and da⸺ ⸺er allusions which open and close the poem. Thematically, it substa⸺ ⸺tes our suspicion that Harold is not altogether anesthetized against emotional stimulants. And finally, it strongly suggests that the narrator's self-imposed exile and his prolonged rationalizations about its justification are merely the retreat and the whimperings of an irresponsible man who wishes to avoid the obligations contingent upon maturity and parenthood. That he can feel deeply and affectionately is indisputable: his bond to "one soft breast" has been tested by "mortal enmities" and cemented by peril; that he recognizes the existence of humanity, the child of his own flesh, and that one "pure love" prefigures at once the mass of fertility images about to be introduced and the narrator's eventual responses to their meaning. Still, the passage is characterized by an ominous tone of finality and a strong sense of Harold's self-deprecating misery. Although the lines are offered to that "one fond breast," no trace of optimism lightens Harold's tone: memory of his loved ones at this point motivates only a deeper lapse into gloom.

But, paradoxically, the stanzas on the "Castled crag of Drachenfels" provide momentary relief from the anguish of introspection. Structurally framed by references to the Rhine's nobly swelling "breast of waters," the stanzas, strewn throughout with figures of life, growth, and process, stress the speaker's suddenly revived responsiveness to Nature's offerings, his capacity for sensory perception of the multifarious manifestations of natural elegance. The beauties of the Rhine valley have reawakened latent affective responses within the speaker: his grief and despair are for the moment obscured by his concentration upon Nature and upon his love for the "thou" to whom the lines are addressed.

After two stanzas on General Marceau (lvi–lvii), who, as opposed to Napoleon, had kept the "whiteness of his soul" by not overstepping Freedom's charter, and one stanza (lviii) on the tower of Ehrenbreitstein, the speaker attempts to leave the Rhine valley, noting that were it not for the *"ceaseless vultures"* which prey "On *self-condemning bosoms,"* (cf. st. xv), Nature might assuage the pain of the despondent heart. Here Nature "Is to the mellow Earth as Autumn to the year." E. H. Coleridge glosses this difficult passage: "as in autumn, the golden mean between summer and winter, the year is at its full; so in the varied scenery of the Rhine there is a harmony of opposites, a combination of beauty."[28] The fundamental issue, however, is the conditional character of the lines: "it *were* here,"

28. *PW*, II, 252, note 2.

Harold insists, that Nature might bequeath man its own harmony, *if it were not* for the "ceaseless vultures." Under the influence of the Drachenfels stanzas, Harold clearly perceives the unifying capability of the Rhine to harmonize the animate and the inanimate, the dynamic and the static; the valley joins

>   in one attaching maze
> The brilliant, fair, and soft,—the glories of old days,
>
> The negligently grand, the fruitful bloom
>   Of coming ripeness, the white city's sheen,
>   The rolling stream, the precipice's gloom,
>   The forest's growth, the Gothic walls between,—
>   The wild rocks shaped as they had turrets been,
>   In mockery of man's art; and these withal
>   A race of faces happy as the scene,
>   Whose fertile bounties here extend to all,
> Still springing o'er thy banks . . . .
>   (sts. lx–lxi)

But Harold is distinct from this "maze;" and his separateness characteristically inspires him to seek some more spectacular object for identification. The very stillness and commonness of the Rhine valley are unsatisfactory to his "unquiet bosom." He therefore turns to the Alps.

The apostrophe to the "Palaces of Nature," and Harold's attempted identification with them, recall in tone and imagery the statements of stanza lv, and the effect upon the speaker is the same now as then: the "vast walls" here "pinnacled *in the clouds their snowy scalps,* / And throned Eternity in *icy halls* / Of *cold sublimity.*" The narrator's emotional response is, predictably, a redoubtable awareness of "How Earth may *pierce* to Heaven, yet leave vain man below." Belittled and intimidated by the majesty of the Alps, therefore, he shrinks immediately back to the plain, reflects briefly upon the contrast between the righteous cause which led to unlimited slaughter at Morat, and the human sacrifices to ambition and lust for power at Waterloo and Cannae, and gradually, still as an after-effect of his thwarted identification with the mountains, again turns inward upon himself. Describing a "lonelier column" of a "gray and grief-worn aspect of old days"—that is, a column from the temple of

Apollo—Harold unconsciously observes in it his own reflection: it is "the last remnant of the *wreck* of years," and appears to him as "one *to stone converted* by amaze, / Yet still with consciousness." We have already witnessed Harold's wish to adopt this stony aspect, to make himself invulnerable both to time and to passion. His projection here confirms his rebuff by the Alps and suggests, possibly, his retreat from recent recollection of his absent lover.

Memory of that lover, in contrast to his identification with the stone column, immediately motivates his elegiac tribute to Julia Alpinula, "a young Aventian princess," Byron's note to the passage explains, who "died soon after a vain endeavor to save her father, condemned as a traitor." The firmness of the bond between father and daughter, and the pathos of their separation, register upon the narrator's sensitivity; and the last line of the stanza presages Harold's spiritual union with his daughter at the conclusion of the poem: their tomb "held within . . . one mind—one heart—one dust." The insertion of these lines at this point, I believe, constitutes further evidence of the speaker's emotional tie to his loved ones, his evolving awareness of the meaning of human relationships.

The next ten stanzas (lxvii–lxxvi) include Harold's tortured rationalizations about the justification for solitude and his efforts to lose himself in the natural environment. A glance at the Alps only reminds him again of their imperishable purity "beyond all things below;" the "mirror" of Lake Leman instigates his carping about overpopulation and his own "unfitness" to mingle with the "herd" (cf. st. xii). Not "discontent," he insists, but this same unfitness forces him

> to keep the mind
> Deep in its *fountain, lest it overboil*
> In the hot throng, where we become the *spoil*
> Of our infection . . . .
>
> (st. lxix)

Among mankind, he continues in the same vein, our souls may be blighted, the "race of life" may be merely a *"hopeless flight;"* and in an image recalling the "empty hull" of stanza xxii, he seems to specify himself as one of many "wanderers o'er Eternity / Whose bark drives on and on, and anchored ne'er shall be." He argues that in communal life we have no opportunity for objectivity, no capacity for analysis or judgment. That Harold devotes so much space and energy to these arguments posits, I think, his uncertainty about their validity. Unsure and discontent, he searches for rational justification. Correspondingly, he tends more toward questions than firm statements of conviction: "Is it not better," he inquires, "to be alone," to reside by the "arrowy Rhone,"

> Or the *pure bosom of its nursing Lake,*
> *Which feeds it as a mother who doth make*
> *A fair but froward infant her own care,*
> Kissing its cares away as these awake . . .?
> (st. lxxi)

Significantly, the parent-child relationship remains central in the speaker's mind; Harold must, therefore, frame his rationalizations as rhetorical questions. Though not convinced of the desirability of abandoning solitude, he is decidedly more inclined at this point than ever before to evaluate seriously the therapeutic advantages inherent in human relationships.

The following four stanzas (lxxii–lxxv) would seem materially to confirm the notion that Harold does manage to merge and mingle with some universal principle embodied in Nature. He claims to become a "portion" of all around him, to receive a "feeling" from the mountains, to be tortured by the "hum / Of human cities." He can see "Nothing to loathe in Nature," *except,* crucially, "to be / A link reluctant in a fleshly chain"—to be a creature of flesh possessed by an aspiring soul which would flee

> And with the *sky*—the *peak*—the *heaving plain*
> *Of Ocean, or the stars,* mingle—and not in vain.
> (st. lxxii)

Declaring his own "absorption" into such natural phenomena, he observes the "peopled *desert past,*" and *anticipates* the day when he can

> *remount* at last
> With a fresh pinion; which I feel to spring,

> Though young, yet waxing vigorous as the Blast
> Which it would cope with, on delighted wing,
> *Spurning the clay-cold bonds which round our being cling.*
>
> (st. lxxiii)

Now the phrase "at last" should be paralleled with the phrase "at length" in stanza lxxiv: Harold is prophesying, hoping, not in fact describing what he presently experiences. "When *at length* the mind shall be all free / From what it hates in this degraded form," he questions, "*shall* I not / Feel all I see?" Admittedly, he recognizes the existence of the "Spirit of each spot," and goes so far as to claim an occasional "share in the immortal lot;" but sense of the body remains heavily upon him, and he turns immediately to perplexed questioning, again in order to convince himself that what he desires is in fact his. He wishes to know definitely that the "mountains, waves, and skies" are a part of him and of his soul, that he should "contemn / All objects," that he ought to isolate himself from the "hard and worldly phlegm" of humanity. Harold's efforts to lose himself in these lines—so marked by manifest incertitude—are, I believe, exercises in desperate self-assurance. As E. H. Coleridge remarks, "Nature and Humanity are antagonists, and he cleaves to the one, yea, he would take her by violence, to mark his alienation and severance from the other."[29] Objections that Harold's remark, "I share at times the immortal lot," is indisputable evidence of his spiritual experiences should be modified by recognition of the narrator's arduous struggle to obtain what was both fantastically brief and altogether unsatisfactory.

The abrupt (and embarrassed?) dismissal of his "spiritual communion" as irrelevant and his prompt shift to a study of Rousseau, whose Nature-mysticism was irrefutable, validates the shallowness and inadequacy of Harold's experiences. Stanzas lxxvi–lxxxi delineate in some detail the character of that "self-torturing sophist, wild Rousseau,"[30] and stress throughout the fire and passion of his spirit

29. *Ibid.,* 262, note 1.

30. "Byron's ambivalence [toward Rousseau] is a necessary consequence of the extraordinary view of the natural world that *Childe Harold's Pilgrimage* develops. Every element given to man is simultaneously a way to moral greatness and divine blessing, and also a quicker way to self-deception and damnation. Every human act that widens consciousness increases both exaltation and despair" (Bloom, p. 236).

and the fatality which such a composition guaranteed. We are advised to "look on One, whose *dust was once all fire,*" one who could cast

> O'er erring deeds and thoughts, a heavenly hue
> Of words, like *sunbeams, dazzling* as they past
> The eyes, which o'er them shed tears feelingly and fast.
>
> (st. lxxvii)

He was like a tree *"On fire by lightning";* he was both *"kindled"* and *"blasted"* by an *"ethereal flame."* But, most importantly, he was enamoured of "ideal Beauty,"

> which became
> In him existence, and o'erflowing teems
> Along his *burning page,* distempered though it seems.
>
> (st. lxxviii)

This "Passion's essence" invested *Julie* with life, accounted for his own *"fevered lip,"* the flash of *"love-devouring heat"* through "brain and breast," and the "oracles which *set the world in flame.*" The fundamental point here is that Rousseau, even in his revolutionary tracts, was so consumed by an elemental flame of desire for the ideal that he remained almost totally foreign to reality, isolated from and oblivious to the limited capacities of human nature. The disparity between the intensity of Rousseau's inspiration and the demonstrable ineffectiveness of his accomplishments strikes Harold as explicable only as the inevitable frustration of a soul which overreaches the limitations of mortality. The speaker is not critical of Rousseau—on the contrary he admires the force of his works—but his appraisal of the Frenchman contains a note of objectivity heretofore largely absent in Harold's evaluations of heroes. Harold no doubt discerns within himself the faults—excessive aloofness, extravagant love for the ideal, preference for solitude—which ensured Rousseau's *"phrensied"* condition. The identification of Harold with Rousseau is here, surely; but the effort at conscious self-criticism is a new and important development.

In lines again echoing the earlier images of the lifeless tree, the empty hull, etc., Harold now inquires:

> What deep wounds ever closed without a scar?
> The heart's bleed longest, and but heal to wear
> That which disfigures it; and *they who war*
> *With their own hopes,* and have been vanquished, bear
> Silence, but not submission . . . .
>
> (st. lxxxiv)

Summarizing the errors of the revolutionaries—particularly Rousseau —he credits them all to the elemental conflict raging within their souls and by implication recalls the battle continuing in his own mind.

Cognizance of the intensity of that war leads him yet again to seek relief in natural beauty. In the next twenty stanzas (lxxxv–civ) occurs Harold's most lengthy and most strenuous effort to assimilate to himself the charm of his environment, to fit himself somehow into the order and harmony and continuity of Nature. The structural location of these stanzas is important: we are approaching the emotional climax of the poem—the point at which Harold must once and for all abandon his consistently thwarted attempts to hurl himself into animate or inanimate objects of identification. But Harold will not give up his endeavors until he has approximated—as nearly as one of his constitution can—a union with some universally binding principle. He cannot forego one final and almost successful bid for Nature's blessings; and his failure is all the more spectacular, his collapse all the more crashing, because of the nearness of his success.

To begin with, we should observe that the thought of his absent loved ones lingers perceptibly in Harold's consciousness: the "soft murmuring" of Lake Leman "Sounds sweet as . . . a Sister's voice;" the "fragrance from the shore" is of "flowers yet fresh with childhood," and the grasshopper is a creature "who makes / His life an infancy." But that recollection is temporarily screened by the attempted identification with the stars (cf. stanza xiv):

> —'tis to be forgiven,
> That in our aspirations to be great,
> Our *destinies o'erleap their mortal state,*
> And *claim a kindred with you;* for ye are
> A Beauty and a Mystery, and create
> In us such love and reverence from afar,

That Fortune,—Fame,—Power,—Life, have named
themselves a Star.
(st. lxxxviii)

Consciousness of the body-soul dichotomy arouses a pang of despair for the moment, but Harold is soon moved to a contemplation—not rapturous, by any means—of the stillness, the breathlessness, of the evening. Everything from the stars to the coast of the lake "is concentered in a life intense," and Harold indeed senses the harmony of the scene. But this is no new or extraordinary experience; he perceived exactly the same thing and felt precisely the same way in the Rhine valley. Harold is impressed with the apparent unity of Nature, but, significantly, he does not affiliate himself with the scheme of things as he observes it.

No one can deny that Harold experiences something very close to mystical ecstasy in the famous ninetieth stanza, but several subtle qualifications in the passage merit close attention. First, the sense of self remains strong: though the "feeling infinite" stirs Harold deeply, he at no point seems to merge or mingle with it. Second, this "truth" "makes known / Eternal harmony," but it never absorbs the speaker into itself; it "sheds a charm," but it does not dissolve Harold's awareness either of the scene or of himself. Third, the speaker's passivity here, in contrast to his spirited participation in the storm a few moments later, argues that he profits little, if at all, from this encounter. If he has throughout sought a cure for ennui, a stimulus for action, his experience here is singularly ineffective. Fourth, the thought of the "spectre Death" at such a moment seems to indicate that Harold has achieved no mystical elevation. Clearly enough, he glimpses a harmony and an order and a oneness in Nature; but, I think, the experience is not rapturous, it is remarkably short-lived, and, as the next stanzas indicate, it is finally disappointing.

The spell is physically shattered by a spectacular thunderstorm which elicits from Harold's sensibilities a response very different from that induced by the "feeling infinite." Masculine strength, deafening sound, and brilliant, blinding light are the kinesthetic keynotes of the passage: everything, including Harold, is suddenly and ecstatically alive. The crags rattle, the thunder "leaps," the Alps are "joyous," the lake "shines, a phosphoric sea," the rain dances, and the "loud hills" shake with "mountain-mirth." Harold, enchanted with it all, yearns to be

> A sharer in thy fierce and far delight,—
> A portion of the tempest . . . .
>
> (st. xciii)

He yearns, but cannot accomplish the identification. For as he gazes upward at two cliffs between which the "swift Rhone cleaves his way," they appear to him "as lovers who have parted" in a foolish rage the very root of which was love—parted only to blight "their life's bloom," and hence to suffer *"an age / Of years all winters,— war within themselves to wage."* That Harold should think thus in terms of human relationships, especially of parted lovers, indicates at once his failure to find satisfaction or release in Nature and his awareness of the importance of human influence in any balanced, mature existence. Notice, too, the speaker's stress upon the "war within;" his own spirit, still battling with itself, weighs heavily upon his consciousness.

After further marveling over the splendor of the lightning, Harold, as the storm abates, shrinks back into himself:

> the far roll
> Of your departing voices, is the knoll
> Of what in me is sleepless . . . .
>
> (st. xcvi)

And he wonders if these storms are

> like those within the human breast?
> Or do ye find, at length, like *eagles,* some high nest?
>
> (st. xcvi)

The haunting knowledge of his tempest-wrought bosom and of his dissimilarity to eagles occasion once again Harold's self-pitying reflections on his inability to rid himself of tormenting thoughts:

> Could I embody and unbosom now
>   That which is most within me,—could I wreak
> My thoughts upon expression, and thus throw
>   Soul—heart—mind—passions—feelings—strong or weak—

> All that I would have sought, and all I seek,
> Bear, know, feel—and yet breathe—into *one*[31] word,
> And that one word were *Lightning,* I would speak;
> But as it is, I live and die unheard,
> With a most voiceless thought, *sheathing it as a sword.*
>
> (st. xcvii)

After Harold's exhausting efforts to assimilate into himself, to become one with the natural spectacles he has just witnessed, this withdrawal and introverted agony are, perhaps, psychologically justifiable. I would emphasize, however, his idolatry of the lightning. The strength, the energy, the voltaic potency of the lightning are the characteristics he yearns throughout the poem to rediscover for himself.

Dejected yet again, Harold can progress in only one direction; and the next seven stanzas (xcviii–civ) are devoted to an elaborate panegyric on the splendor of the Clarens countryside. But a decided difference distinguishes this passage from former descriptions of similar scenes. The opening lines of stanza xcix strike the new note: "Clarens! sweet Clarens [,] birthplace of deep Love!" The universal, life-giving principle is everywhere evidenced, and Harold catalogues its manifestations with unaccustomed gusto. Moreover, not once in these stanzas is there the vitiating intrusion of a column, a stone monument, a decaying castle, a lonely graveyard; all is growth and process and development and animation. "Trees take root in Love;" the glaciers and crags (formerly symbols of haughty isolation and cold pride) speak now of Love; and, most revealingly, the "tender power" of Love "Passes the strength of storms in their most desolate hour." "All things are here of *Him:*"[32] pines, torrents, vines, and woods. Recalling for us the former image of the withered tree, the speaker now surveys

> The covert of old trees, with trunks all hoar,
> But *light leaves, young as joy, stands where it stood.*
>
> (st. ci)

The place is populous with "bees and birds," "fearless and full of

31. Byron's emphasis.
32. Byron's emphasis.

life," and the "gush of springs," the "fall of lofty fountains," the "stirring branches," and the fresh "bud" all invest the scene with a vitality which Harold senses strongly and acknowledges enthusiastically. But still more significantly, Harold seems at last to grasp the demands which Love places upon his disciples: it is Love's "nature"

> to advance or die;
> He stands not still, but or decays, or grows
> Into a boundless blessing, which may vie
> With the immortal lights, in its eternity!
>   (st. ciii)

The stultifying effect of standing still, or of reveling in retrospection, or of viewing the future with bleak forebodings, has perhaps finally registered upon Harold. To be informed with Love, it would seem, is to assuage or at least mitigate the anguish of the breast, and, perhaps, after all, to challenge the stars.[33]

So Harold turns confidently to the Alps, determined to *"pierce"* the clouds above them and "survey what'er / May be permitted." He is neither intimidated by their majesty nor deterred by their height; he is moving, acting, advancing, apparently no longer a slave to ennui. Similarly, he views Italy as the "fount at which the panting Mind assuages / Her thirst of knowledge, quaffing there her fill." The implication of the lines is that he sets his sights on "Rome's imperial hill," there also to reactivate his lethargic spirit.

But all of this action, self-assurance, optimism, and determination is eclipsed by stanza cxi, which seems to represent Harold deprived of all he has gained through suffering:

> Thus far have I proceeded in a theme
> Renewed with no kind auspices:—to feel
> We are not what we have been, and to deem
> We are not what we should be,—and to steel

33. Stanzas cv–cvii briefly characterize Voltaire and Gibbon, both men "who sought and found, by dangerous roads, / A path to perpetuity of Fame," both of "Titan-like" minds who risked Heaven's wrath in their quest for knowledge. Harold, however, makes no effort to identify himself with them, nor to judge their products (the condemnation of l. 1002 is negated by the following stanza). He has presumably outgrown the need to do so.

> The heart against itself; and to conceal
> With a proud caution, love, or hate, or aught,—
> Passion or feeling, purpose, grief, or zeal,—
> Which is the tyrant Spirit of our thought,
> Is a stern task of soul:—No matter,—it is taught.
>
> (st. cxi)

As a matter of fact, it is *not* taught. Harold is manifestly lying. He has throughout the poem struggled to "steel / The heart against itself," but he has utterly and absolutely failed. Now, on the very brink of returning to society, of recognizing the claims of emotion and passion, he recoils in horror from risking again the possible agony of a broken heart. He has repeatedly felt, repeatedly admitted the value of Love; but he withdraws once more, and for three more stanzas rationalizes the desirability of isolation.

All, however, is not quite lost; Harold's quest will continue, for, though he has "found them not," he yet believes that there are genuine "hopes" and "Virtues:"

> I would also deem
> O'er others' griefs that some sincerely grieve—
> That two, or one, are almost what they seem,—
> That Goodness is no name—and Happiness no dream.
>
> (st. cxiv)

This is a reluctant and cautious statement of faith; but as though to verify his convictions on the matter, Harold's thought returns to his daughter. None, he confesses, "Can be so wrapt in thee" as he is himself:

> To aid thy mind's development,—to watch
> Thy dawn of little joys,—to sit and see
> Almost thy very growth,—to view thee catch
> Knowledge of objects,—wonders yet to thee!
> To hold thee lightly on a gentle knee,
> And print on thy soft cheek a parent's kiss,—
> This, it should seem, was not reserved for me—
> Yet this was in my nature:—as it is,
> I know not what is there, yet something like to this.
>
> (st. cxvi)

The parental interest in the growth and development of the child—though ironically and paradoxically opposed to the growth and development we should have liked to see in Harold himself—is an admirable and redeeming quality, and at least the narrator admits that "something like to this" is still a part of his character. The admission of course belies his claim to have steeled his heart against affection. At the same time, however, his confession and his assurance that the child will love him is not a strong enough impetus to force Harold back to humanity. Although willing to "waft" a "blessing" to the child, Harold refuses to accept the responsibilities and obligations of Love. He has, nevertheless, advanced substantially, for he does now understand that although a "man may reject his civilization," he "cannot reject his humanity."[34] The love for the daughter is Harold's only remaining tie to humankind, and it is the one thing that keeps him alive. He has been reawakened to the meaning of love; he manifests a spiritual and emotional union with his daughter; his responsiveness to affective stimuli has been thoroughly restored; and he is unquestionably vulnerable now both to "grief" and "gladness."

I I I

The number, the thoroughness, and the ingenuity of critiques on *Manfred*[35] notwithstanding, one is tempted finally to accept Byron's shrugging estimate that his "dramatic poem" of 1817 was "of a very wild, metaphysical, and inexplicable kind."[36] We may nevertheless distill from various interpretations a tentative thematic statement to which most readers might subscribe: burdened by a nameless guilt,

34. Kroeber, p. 138.

35. A definitive listing of these is not practical here, but in addition to studies by Lovell, Kroeber, Marshall, Rutherford, Bostetter, and Bloom already cited in this chapter, I have found the following analyses also especially useful: Samuel C. Chew, *The Dramas of Lord Byron* (New York: Russell & Russell, 1964 [reissued]); Bertrand Evans, "Manfred's Remorse and Dramatic Tradition," *PMLA*, LXII (1947), 752–773; G. Wilson Knight, "The Two Eternities: An Essay on Byron," in *The Burning Oracle* (New York: Oxford University Press, 1939); E. W. Marjarum, *Byron as Skeptic and Believer* (Princeton: Princeton University Press, 1938); and Paul West, *Byron and the Spoiler's Art* (New York: St. Martin's Press, 1960).

36. Letter to Murray, 15 February 1817; *L & J*, IV, 54–55.

tormented by an insatiable thirst for knowledge, and damned by the aspiring impulses of his imagination, Manfred impiously violates the prescribed boundaries of mortal learning in an effort to assert the supremacy of his own mind and hence sever his link with humanity. Seeking to obliterate sensuous awareness, Manfred strives at the same time for a redefinition of his spiritual identity by stripping himself of dependence upon all elements external to himself. Byron of course insists here as elsewhere upon the autonomy of the titanic mind, "not its freedom from moral laws, but its independence of any system of rewards and punishments administered by an external power, and the impossibility of its escaping from the mental consequences of its sins, which must simply be accepted and endured."[37] But only after repeatedly thwarted attempts to project himself into spectacular natural and preternatural phenomena does Manfred learn to rely solely upon the Promethean toughness of his own mental fiber and to find satisfaction in affirming, through his terminal defiant act, the immunity of human will to inferior powers. In a series of ritualistic colloquies,[38] Manfred receives and contemptuously rejects various alternatives to independence; after each rejection "he is forced more consciously back upon himself, and the inevitability of self-responsibility is revealed."[39]

The image patterns of the play, similar to those in the Third Canto of *Childe Harold's Pilgrimage,* are here organized and controlled by the central configuration of the counterpart. Galled by the restricting and inhibiting properties of the "clay" body, Manfred seeks self-fulfillment and completion by identifying himself with objects which possess qualities or faculties denied to him: the untrammeled flight of the eagle, the "life and warmth" of the sun, the spontaneous energy of tempests and cataracts and avalanches and earthquakes, the "gentler powers" of Astarte, and the infinite knowledge, as he thinks, of mysterious supernatural creatures. His attempted projections, of course, exhaust and dismay the hero, even while they dramatize for him the futility of searching for sustenance outside the individual psyche. In any case, the multiple counterpart images are fundamen-

37. Rutherford, p. 88.
38. Bostetter, p. 281.
39. *Ibid.*

tally appurtenant to theme, structure, and characterization in *Manfred*.

Parts of the "Preface" to *Alastor* are useful to a study of *Manfred:* the poem, says Shelley,

represents a youth of . . . adventurous genius led forth by an imagination inflamed . . . through familiarity with all that is excellent and majestic, to the contemplation of the universe. He drinks deep of the fountains of knowledge, and is still insatiate. The magnificence and beauty of the external world sinks profoundly into the frame of his conceptions, and affords to their modifications a variety not to be exhausted. . . . His mind . . . thirsts for intercourse with an intelligence similar to itself. He images to himself the Being he loves. Conversant with speculations of the sublimest and most perfect natures, the vision in which he embodies his own imaginations unites all of wonderful, or wise, or beautiful, which the poet, the philosopher, or the lover could depicture. The intellectual faculties, the imagination, the function of sense have their respective requisitions on the sympathy of corresponding powers in other human beings. The Poet is represented as uniting these requisitions, and attaching them to a single image. He seeks in vain for a prototype of his conception.[40]

Shelley's Poet and Byron's Manfred are of course far from identical on all counts; but a chief similarity between the two is their attempt to objectify an imaginary vision of the ideal that embodies all the wonder of a poet, the wisdom of a philosopher, and the beauty of a lover and their attempt to accomplish this realization without sacrificing their basic individualities entirely to it. In other words, this archetypal ideal must incorporate all the poet's faculties, and, simultaneously, at the moment of conception, be a perfect mirror of the poet's personality: the created and the creator are complementary counterparts of each other. But to "imagine" and to "realize" this vision are separate and perhaps self-contradictory exercises, although to the Poet and to Manfred, the first necessitates an attempt at the second—an attempt destined to failure by the impossibility of concretizing an ideal.

A desire for self-realization by way of identification with an extrapersonal counterpart presupposes, of course, a fragmentation of or at

40. *The Complete Works of Percy Bysshe Shelley,* edited by Roger Ingpen and Walter E. Peck, 10 vols. (New York: Scribner's, 1926–1930), I, 473.

least a deficiency in the individual. The consummate egoism of the typical romantic does not contradict such a sense of inadequacy, for mortal existence, insofar as it falls short of a visionary ideal, cannot be unconditionally accepted. Similarly, if the romantic recognizes his imperfection and strives to improve that condition according to the pattern of his prototypal conception, he is bound to view his present state with a sense of guilt—bound to feel remorse over his shortcomings. E. H. Coleridge established a useful, though somewhat limited, view of the drama that possibly needs modification: "the *motif* of *Manfred* is remorse—eternal suffering for inexpiable crime."[41] Although Coleridge did not find (or did not admit to finding) an illicit love motif in the drama, nearly everyone since has insisted that the Byron-Augusta Leigh affair is unnervingly imaged in the Manfred-Astarte relationship, and has axiomatically assumed that Manfred's guilt is rooted in incest. The incest theme cannot be blinked away; but a biographical reading of the play fails to answer large and troublesome questions. Hence, to my mind, the motivation behind Manfred's search for "self-oblivion" is not so much a guilt over illicit love as it is a more generalized remorse over an unfulfilled potentiality: frustrated attempts to realize within himself the perfectibility embodied in the imagined ideal have bred in him paranoiac self-reproach.

Complete realization of his own identity thus thwarted, Manfred attempts a partial metamorphosis into some*one* else or some*thing* else, his purpose being, of course, to assimilate to himself whatever he can (or all he can) of the good, the true, and the beautiful from the object of identification. These objects, or counterparts, are of two kinds, elemental and supra-personal, but are analogous insofar as they represent idealized components of the hero's personality. Primary among Manfred's drives is his voracious hunger for knowledge beyond the limits of human ratiocination. Confined by the "clankless chain" of humanity—the inhibiting cell of clay—the aspiring impulse invokes "Spirits of earth and air." Twice his invocation (I, i) elicits no response; but on the third trial, Manfred resorts to

> a power,
> Deeper than all yet urged, a tyrant-spell,

41. *PW*, IV, 82.

> Which had its birthplace in a star condemned,
> The burning wreck of a demolished world,
> A wandering hell in the eternal Space . . . .
> (I, i, 42–46)

Revealing the damned and disintegrating qualities of Manfred's character, the imagery of the passage also emphasizes the desires which still burn within the "wreck." Observe, too, the hero's characterization of himself as a "star condemned": anticipating the repeated references throughout the drama to planets, comets, meteors, and other astronomical phenomena, the star-figure suggests Manfred's similarity to a fallen angel, presently reduced to a deplorably low estate but still cognizant of the sublimity which was (or should have been) his.

The Seven Spirits (the "mind and principle" of the elements) respond now to Manfred's adjuration, although they are visible only in the shape of a single, stationary star. In their respective speeches, the spirits delineate their distinctive qualities, whether these be beauty (Cloud and Ocean), height (Mountain), energy (Earth and Wind), or mystery (Night). The figures of height and depth and eruptive or destructive forces, however, ominously foreshadow the speech of the Seventh Spirit (Manfred's star), and hence offer an oblique though significant comment on the hero's character. In a passage recalling Manfred's earlier self-characterization, the last spirit describes the cosmic upheaval at some undetermined point in the past and the effect of that cataclysm on Manfred's star:

> it became
> A wandering mass of shapeless flame,
> A pathless Comet, and a curse,
> The menace of the Universe;
> Still rolling on with innate force,
> Without a sphere, without a course,
> A bright deformity on high,
> The monster of the upper sky!
> And Thou! beneath its influence born—
> Thou worm!
> (I, i, 116–125)

This, then, is Manfred's inescapable heritage: the victim of a galactic catastrophe, he shares with this careening comet its incandescence, its lack of direction, its fatality, its "deformity," and its anomaly among its kind.

Conscious of his dilemma (the blazing imagination imprisoned in clay), Manfred requires of these spirits not additional knowledge, but "Forgetfulness . . . Oblivion—self-oblivion!" referring, in one way, to obliteration of the physical self. He desires the unqualified release of his imaginative faculties: "The Mind—the Spirit—the Promethean spark, / The lightning of my being, is as bright, / Pervading, and far darting as your own, / And shall not yield to yours, though cooped in clay!" Paradoxically, this "lightning"—the motivation of Manfred's imaginative flights—also occasions his demand for "forgetfulness"—that is, a cancellation of his vision of the ideal. So long as this spiritual aspiration is thwarted by the physical body, the "continuance of enduring thought" provides only torture. The important issue here is that although unanswered and unsatisfied by the seven spectres, the imaginative faculty in Manfred's character dramatically responds to their forceful speeches, while his physical nature demands visualization of the ideal which they represent. Complying with his wish, the Seventh Spirit appears "in the shape of a beautiful female figure" but, significantly, upon Manfred's attempt to clasp her, she vanishes (cf., "But my embrace was fatal"). Clearly, this spectre, if not an early premonition of the Astarte-figure, does represent the non-physical ideal toward which Manfred strives. She is, moreover, a portion of Manfred's own character which was itself fractured at that "all nameless hour," that instant of time noted in the speech of the Seventh Spirit. The time alluded to here is, perhaps, a kind of Blakean moment of creation in which the individual personality as it existed in a precreative state was fragmented into various parts; but subsequently each part of that personality retained some recollection of the unity it had once known. Hence, the "awful chaos—light and darkness, / And mind and dust; and passions and pure thoughts, / Mixed, and contending without end or order." From such recollection evolves also the "conflict" of the "elements" which lacks an organizing principle in physical existence. And the figure in this early scene may well be the female counterpart to the male Manfred. The hero's act of clasping her to himself thus becomes symbolic of his attempt to re-establish that fundamental unity broken at birth.

Such a theory is supported by the fatalism under which Manfred operates. Deterministic elements appear as early as the hero's first speech, but a curse is inflicted squarely and explicitly upon him only after his thwarted attempt to embrace the female figure. The curse itself echoes precisely Manfred's own presentiment of his fate: "Nor to slumber, nor to die, / Shall be thy destiny." Accompanying the malediction is an oppressive catalogue of images (ll. 192–261) designed to suggest the unfathomable mystery of the universal conspiracy launched against the hero:

> From thy false tears I did distil
> An essence which hath strength to kill;
> From thy own heart I then did wring
> The black blood in its blackest spring;
> From thy own smile I snatched the snake,
> For there it coiled as in a brake;
> From thy own lip I drew the charm
> Which gave all these their chiefest harm;
> In proving every poison known,
> I found the strongest was thine own.
>
> By thy cold breast and serpent smile,
> By thy unfathomed gulfs of guile,
> By that most seeming virtuous eye,
> By thy shut soul's hypocrisy;
> By the perfection of thine art
> Which passed for human thine own heart;
> By thy delight in others' pain,
> And by thy brotherhood of Cain,
> I call upon thee! and compel
> Thyself to be thy proper Hell!
>   (I, i, 232–251)

Many of these figures Byron obviously lifted from the stock of the graveyard school of poetry, but their cumulative effect here, in conveying the enigmatic fatality of Manfred's existence, is singularly appropriate: all of them produce the desired effect of inescapable damnation. From this point on, then, and possibly from his birth, the hero's actions are determined by a fate over which he apparently has no control, one which he has provoked by his ambitious, self-assertive act in the former scene. The struggle becomes dual: Manfred with his divided self, and Manfred against a malign destiny.

Despite the protagonist's avowals of forthright individualism, the disappearance of the suprapersonal counterpart leaves him wanting; and he shifts his projections to the immensities and otherwise startling aspects of the natural world. Discovered alone upon the Jungfrau, he substitutes natural phenomena for superhuman aid, because the strength of the mountains, the expansiveness of the sky, the flame of the sun, and the force of the avalanche feed a primitive hunger in Manfred, while at the same time mirroring the vigor of his quest, the scope of his desire, the burning of his aspirations, and the self-destructiveness of his mission. From his precarious perch at the edge of a precipice, he spots a "cloud-cleaving" eagle; already contemplating suicide, he says, "I should be / Thy prey, and gorge thine eaglets," but his identification with the bird is clear enough:

> thou art gone
> Where the eye cannot follow thee; but thine
> Yet pierces downward, onward, or above,
> With a pervading vision. —Beautiful!
> How beautiful is all this visible world!
> (I, ii, 33–37)

The projection into the eagle-counterpart—its soaring flight, its pervading vision, its un-mortal life—is almost instantaneous, for no sooner has Manfred identified imaginatively with the bird than the physical or "lower" essence summons back the spirit, and his "Mortality predominates." Now occurs Byron's most explicit statement on the cause of the human predicament: we who would call ourselves the "sovereigns" of earth are in fact

> Half dust, half deity, alike unfit
> To sink or soar, with our mixed essence make
> A conflict of its elements, and breathe
> The breath of degradation and of pride,
> Contending with low wants and lofty will,
> Till our Mortality predominates,
> And men are—what they name not to themselves.
> (I, ii, 40–46)

This is a cry of pathetic bewilderment and despair over what course of action is open to men so constituted of dust and deity, so wracked apart by the antithetical impulses of their beings. The polarities of mortal existence receive their most eloquent, if most concentrated, expression in these lines, and the passage is crucial to Byron's entire canon. In Manfred's particular case, cognizance of his quandary prompts him, impetuously, to make another effort at the total disembodiment of his spirit:

> Oh, that I were
> The viewless [i.e., invisible] spirit of a lovely sound,
> A living voice, a breathing harmony,
> A bodiless enjoyment—born and dying
> With the blest tone which made me!
> (I, ii, 52–56)

But the transmutation of the spirit into a "harmony" will not work, and Manfred, exhausted, falls back to self-laceration and dejection. In a series of figures reminiscent of Childe Harold's self-characterization, Manfred sees himself as a "blasted" pine, the spoil of "a single winter," "A blighted trunk upon a cursed root." Unable to bear the strain of such recognition—the intellectual and emotional sterility implicit in his present condition—his endurance dissolves into debilitated cowardice, and he attempts to leap into the chasm below.

Rescued by the Chamois Hunter, Manfred carefully sketches the virtues of a peasant existence, but denies the Hunter as an enviable counterpart to his own life. Possessed of a "scorched" soul, he abandons the Hunter and enters a lower Alpine valley (observe his physical descent from the heights), proposing to "divide / The homage of these waters" with the spirit of a torrential cataract. By invoking the Witch of the Alps, the hero of course breaks his former vow to "lean no more on super-human aid;" even though his first wish is simply to "gaze on thee a moment," the old desires for pardon, forgetfulness, and death are soon reiterated.

But more significant than this minor inconsistency are the visible characteristics of the Witch and her remarkable power to elicit from Manfred the most scrupulously guarded secrets of his soul. First of all, Manfred sees that in the Witch "The charms of Earth's least mortal daughters grow / To an unearthly stature, in an essence / Of purer elements," and finds in her countenance "The blush of earth embracing with her Heaven." This "Beautiful Spirit," then, reminiscent of the figure in Act I, and foreshadowing the appearance of Astarte, combines in physical form spiritual perfection: the elements of earth married with those of heaven. She represents the chimerical counterpart with which the hero yearns to integrate his own personality. Indeed, she is almost Astarte. Furthermore, she draws from Manfred a detailed autobiography, the most important parts of which are particulars about his early life and his characterization of Astarte. Manfred itemizes the course of his existence as a series of attempts to shake off his "breathing flesh," to outstrip, by soaring or plunging, the "creatures of clay" who girded him about:

> My joy was in the wilderness,—to breathe
> The difficult air of the iced mountain's top,
>   . . . or to plunge
> Into the torrent, and to roll along
> On the swift whirl of the new-breaking wave
> Of river-stream, or Ocean, in their flow.
>   . . . or
> To follow through the night the moving moon,
> The stars in their development; or catch
> The dazzling lightnings till my eyes grew dim;
> Or to look, list'ning, on the scattered leaves,
>   . . . I dived,
> In my lone wanderings, to the caves of Death.
>   (II, ii, 62–80)

He begins in the wilderness, ascends to the peaks, plummets to the torrent, rises to the moon, stars, and lightnings, returns to the earth, and plunges at last into subterranean regions—all for nothing. His search for phenomena which would complement and complete what he senses should be his "whole" self has only increased awareness of his deficiency. But the detailed account of his quest and his failures forces upon him the allusion to Astarte, the one salutary counterpart to his personality:

> She was like me in lineaments—her eyes—
> Her hair—her features—all, to the very tone
> Even of her voice, they said were like to mine;
> But softened all, and tempered into beauty:

> She had the same lone thoughts and wanderings,
> The quest of hidden knowledge, and a mind
> To comprehend the Universe: nor these
> Alone, but with them gentler powers than mine,
> Pity, and smiles, and tears—which I had not;
> And tenderness—but that I had for her;
> Humility—and that I never had.
> Her faults were mine—her virtues were her own.
>
> (II, ii, 105–116)

We may, if we must, see Augusta Leigh in these lines; but we must also see Manfred's love for and dependence upon a part of himself disjoined from himself. And his quest throughout the drama is for a reconstruction of the fragmented unity precipitated by Astarte's death.[42]

A single recourse, then, is left to the protagonist: he may summon Astarte from the dead with the intercessory aid of Arimanes and the king's entourage of demonic spirits. Scene iii of Act II opens on the assembling of the Destinies: they gather on moonlit snow "Where never human foot" has trod, where the rugged appearance of the mountains resembles "A tumbling tempest's foam, / Frozen in a moment—a dead Whirlpool's image." Robed in clouds, their "fantastic pinnacle" is "The fretwork of some earthquake." And throughout their respective speeches, the stress is consistently upon universal calamity, wretched suffering, spectacular smash. Furthermore, the "Hymn of the Spirits" to Arimanes in scene iv recalls the earlier description by the Seventh Spirit of the meteoric cataclysm preceding Manfred's birth. In the hand of this "Prince of Earth and Air" is

> The sceptre of the Elements, which tear
>   Themselves to chaos at his high command!
> He breatheth—and a tempest shakes the sea;
>   He speaketh—and the clouds reply in thunder;
> He gazeth—from his glance the sunbeams flee;
>   He moveth—Earthquakes rend the world asunder.
> Beneath his footsteps the Volcanoes rise;

42. Knight also sees Astarte as Manfred's "double, in looks and soul," but his emphasis is upon the rich sexual ambiguity inherent in the figure (pp. 217–219).

> His shadow is the Pestilence: his path
> The comets herald through the crackling skies;
> And Planets turn to ashes at his wrath.
>
> (II, iv, 3–12)

It is entirely fitting, therefore, that Manfred seek assistance from Arimanes, for not only does he owe his wrecked condition to the influence of the Prince, but he also aspires to wield the kind of power, possess the kind of knowledge, and command the kind of recognition characteristic of Arimanes.

Employing all the superhuman apparatus at his disposal, Manfred ascends to the Hall of the Prince, refuses him obeisance, but is defended as one "of no common order." Thus by virtue of his immortal suffering, Manfred is granted communion with the Phantom of Astarte. Of the spirit he requests forgiveness or condemnation for "too much loving;" indeed, it was the "deadliest sin to love as we have loved"—deadly, because all influences antagonistic to their absolute erotic and imaginative identification were excluded and negated through the singularity of their focus upon each other. The separation by death of two inextricably joined spirits left the one impoverished and desperate:

> I have outwatched the stars,
> And gazed o'er heaven in vain search of thee.
> Speak to me! I have wandered o'er the earth,
> And never found thy likeness—Speak to me!
>
> (II, iv, 141–144)

But the Phantom supplies neither forgiveness, nor mercy, nor a reassurance of its love, but only the promise of death; and Manfred, for seeking things beyond mortality, is convulsed.

Nevertheless, the opening scene of Act III finds the hero relatively secure in the guarantee that death will end his earthly ills (ll. 6–18). As he anticipates, however, this is temporary triumph; for all his protestations of independence, for all his rejections of mortal companionship, Manfred is by no means as self-sufficient as he would have us think. His projections into, or identifications with, extra-human elements continue. After refusing the Abbot's offering of divine solace, Manfred once more compares the course of his exist-

ence to "the wind, / The red-hot breath of the most lone Simoon
. . ." which "being met is deadly"—the implication of such remarks
being that he has discovered sympathy in this natural phenomenon.
But most important is his address to the setting sun, his empathic
identification with it in III, ii (a speech that has its ironic counterpart in I, ii, 10ff.). The objects of Manfred's projection in this apostrophe are dual: the sun, with its warmth and energy and divine
aspect, on the one hand; and on the other, "the vigorous race / Of
undiseased mankind, the giant sons / Of the embrace of Angels,
with a sex / More beautiful than they." This "vigorous race," I
think, may refer to mythological or apocryphal creatures, not sexless
like the angels, but containing in themselves both male and female
principles. As I have suggested, Manfred seems to seek this sort of
hermaphroditic oneness; in its absence, guilt consumes him.

Why, then, after futile searches, after numerous unacceptable projections into counterparts, does Manfred find it "not so difficult to
die"? The answer lies not so much in his hope of being reunited with
Astarte as in this speech of defiance to the summoning spectres:

> The Mind which is immortal makes itself
> Requital for its good or evil thoughts,—
> Is its own origin of ill and end—
> And its own place and time: its innate sense,
> When stripped of this mortality, derives
> No colour from the fleeting things without,
> But is absorbed in sufferance or in joy,
> Born from the knowledge of its own desert.
> *Thou* didst not tempt me, and thou couldst not tempt me;
> I have not been thy dupe, nor am thy prey—
> But was my own destroyer, and will be
> My own hereafter.
>   (III, iv, 129–140)

Informing these lines is no search for oblivion, forgetfulness, self-
obliteration; no invocation of any elemental or preternatural powers
for pardon or forgiveness or mercy or love; no rationalization or
pathological whimpering. This is the daring challenge of a man
triumphant over his need to discover fulfillment outside himself. Only
at this instant is Manfred, having accepted the responsibility for his

actions and having admitted the impossibility of deriving comfort from "things without"—only now is he totally independent of extra-personal influences. Realizing to the fullest possible extent the sense of his own independent powers and affirming energetically the autonomy of human character, Manfred can die with comparative ease.

But insistence upon the ultimate triumph or defeat of the hero is fundamentally beside the point. To say, on the one hand, that Manfred is victorious because he is independent at the last of all influences external to the self, or to claim, on the other hand, that he is beaten because he has established no external co-ordinates of the self, is not to argue advantageously or conclusively, given the solipsistic world he has attained at the end of the drama. It is perhaps more meaningful to say that triumph in such a world depends totally upon the individual's own definition and acceptance of self. In the vacuum of Manfred's selfhood, our traditional interpretations of "triumph" and "defeat" are altogether meaningless.

The Haunted Epoch

I will be what I should be, or be nothing.

—*Marino Faliero*

I know not what I could have been, but feel
I am not what I should be.

—*Sardanapalus*

                    Would I ne'er had been
Aught else but dust!

—*Cain*

L ORD BYRON left Switzerland in the fall of 1816. Shortly after his arrival in Italy, he established himself as one of the eminent debauchees and literati of Venice. Enamored of Italy's cultural and political heritage, as well as of its women, he undertook on 25 February 1817 the dramatization of one incident of that history in *Marino Faliero,* but his recent introduction to, and enthusiastic preoccupation with, the works of John Hookham Frere, Luigi Pulci, and Dante (although he had read Dante earlier in translation) delayed completion of the new drama until 17 July 1820.[1] *Marino Faliero* was followed in January 1821 by *Sardanapalus* and in September of the same year by *Cain: A Mystery.* Despite all of his sensual entanglements and his experiments with the Italian satiric tradition, Byron produced five dramas (including *The Two Foscari* and *Heaven and Earth*) in fifteen months.

1. Byron composed all of his so-called "Italian poems" between April 1817 and March 1820: *The Lament of Tasso* (20 April 1817), *Beppo* (6 September–12 October 1817), *Ode on Venice* (July 1818), *The Prophecy of Dante* (June 1819), and the translation of the Francesca de Rimini episode from the Fifth Canto of the *Inferno* (March 1820). We may also recall that the poet rewrote the third act of *Manfred* and completed the Fourth Canto of *Childe Harold's Pilgrimage* after his removal to Venice. Furthermore, he wrote Cantos I through V of *Don Juan* between September 1818 and November 1820. Most commentators agree that Byron's early Italian poems are of interest chiefly for the light they shed on the evolution of *Don Juan.* By themselves, as Paul Elmer More remarks, these poems are probably the "least valuable portion of Byron's work" (*The Complete Poetical Works of Byron* [Cambridge: Houghton Mifflin, 1933], p. 436).

Various commentators have credited Byron's departure from the romantic mode of *Manfred* in favor of the classicism or pseudo-classicism of his later dramas to the influence of Vittorio Alfieri and Vincenzo Monti, with whose works he became acquainted during his visits to Milan and Venice. E. H. Coleridge remarks, "He had been powerfully impressed by the energy and directness of Alfieri's work, and he was eager to emulate the gravity and simplicity, if not the terseness and conciseness, of his style and language."[2] No doubt Byron was forcefully struck by Alfieri's dramas[3] and he consciously determined to imitate Alfieri's dramatic technique in his own work. He was particularly taken with the notion of the three unities, and he bragged excessively about the historical accuracy which he thought his plays reflected. But Byron seems to have believed that the impact of Alfieri's plays depended to a large degree upon the Italian's adherence to the principles of historical accuracy and classical structure. Goethe is said to have "laughed to think that Byron, who, in practical life could never adapt himself, and never even asked about a law, finally subjected himself to the stupidest of laws—that of the *three unities.*"[4] Even though Byron knew the Greek drama from his Cambridge days (if not earlier), the fact of the matter is that he did not understand the function of dramatic structure or the purpose of historical accuracy: his efforts to construct dramas according to the

2. *The Poetical Works of Lord Byron,* edited by Ernest Hartley Coleridge, 7 vols. (London: John Murray, Ltd., 1898–1904), IV, 327; all textual references are to this edition, hereafter cited as *PW.*

3. Note particularly Byron's remark to John Murray in a letter dated 12 August 1819: "Last night I went to the representation of Alfieri's *Mirra,* the last two acts of which threw me into convulsions. I do not mean by that word a lady's hysterics, but the agony of reluctant tears, and the choaking [*sic*] shudder, which I do not often undergo for fiction" *(The Letters and Journals of Lord Byron,* edited by Rowland E. Prothero, 6 vols. [London: John Murray, Ltd., 1898–1904], IV, 339–340, hereafter cited as *L & J).* His *"Dama"* for the evening described his reaction as follows: "Lord Byron took a strong interest in the representation, and it was evident that he was deeply affected. At length there came a point of the performance at which he could no longer restrain his emotions:—he burst into a flood of tears, and, his sobs preventing him from remaining any longer in the box, he rose and left the theater" (quoted in *L & J,* IV, 340, note 1). For other of Byron's references to Alfieri, see *L & J,* IV, 114; V, 64, 81, 218, 323, 372, and 408.

4. Quoted in *PW,* IV, 327.

rules of classical art result in a rigid, nonfunctional structure, imposed from without on the represented events, adding little if anything to the over-all impact of the plays. Byron was partially aware that the real merits of his dramas neither depended upon nor were really related to their formal construction. For all his protests about their regularity and their preservation of the unities, he is steadily conscious of their unfitness for the stage, and he insists that the poetry of them receive due respect. In a letter to Murray (20 September 1820) Byron reminded his editor that *Marino Faliero "never was intended nor written with any view to the Stage. I have said so in the preface too. It is too long and too regular for your stage. The persons too few, and the unity too much observed. It is more like a play of Alfieri's than of your stage (I say this humbly speaking of that great Man); but there is poetry, and it is equal to Manfred."*[5] But if, as I think, Byron was consciously striving to capture the emotional intensity of Alfieri's plays by imitating their classical structure, he was not able entirely to curb his tendency toward extravagant and grandiose poetizing. "It has been my object," he wrote of *Sardanapalus,* "to be as simple and severe as Alfieri, and I have broken down the *poetry* as nearly as I could to common language."[6] Rarely does Byron approximate "common language" in his dramas. Perhaps aware that the action, the characterizations, the fidelity to actual fact, and the preservation of the unities were in his employ insufficient tools to convey emotional power, Byron frequently returned to his forte—the exaggerated, declamatory monologue[7]—hoping it would carry the main burden of dramatic communication.

This is not to suggest that Byron failed to develop a strong sense of stylistic restraint during his experiments with the Italian satiric tradition, for his rhetorical flights in *Marino Faliero, Sardanapalus,* and *Cain* are generally less frequent than was the case in *Manfred.*

5. *L & J,* V, 81.
6. *Ibid.,* 323.
7. As Paul West points out (*Byron and the Spoiler's Art* [New York: St. Martin's Press, 1961]), "Byron, as ever, is more interested in emotions than in ideas, in attitudes rather than motives, in flourish rather than steady observation, in similitudes rather than analysis. . . . The plays really amount to prodigious soliloquies set out as drama. . . . States of mind intrigue him; events hardly at all" (pp. 100–119).

My point is simply that the poetry of these three dramas is by no means less important than their dramatic structure. The poetry is worth studying because it, and not the adherence to classical formulas of construction, empowers the plays with emotional intensity and dramatic strength usually equal, and sometimes superior, to *Manfred*.

Poetic intensity and strength usually arise out of severe crises or wrenching conflicts. By leaving Switzerland, Byron scarcely escaped the mental conflicts which tormented him there, just as Switzerland itself had not much assuaged his memory of English injustices. In the dramas of the Italian period, therefore, Byron searches out historical and Biblical characters who represent not necessarily the warring elements of his own mind, but who at least represent a mind in conflict with itself. It is of course easy enough to find Byron in the aristocratic pride of Marino Faliero, the sybaritic sloth of Sardanapalus, the theosophic questioning of Cain; but the emphasis here is consistently upon the imaginative recreation of situations, characters, and internal struggles with which Byron was not personally familiar, and it is no longer necessary to suppose that he projects himself into his dramatic personages for the purpose of relieving repressed tensions. He may still *write* for this reason. But as I hope to show in the following discussion, he is in these dramas primarily a literary craftsman, an objective technician, carefully molding his characters, his themes, his poetry into a unified dramatic whole.

I

A brief recapitulation of Byron's version[8] of Marino Faliero's history may be appropriate. The play opens with the news that Michel Steno has received an unjustly light sentence from the ruling Forty for scribbling on the ducal throne a vicious insult against the wife of Marino Faliero, Doge of Venice. Believing that the Forty had added insult to injury by its leniency, Marino, in a fit of temper, spurns the ducal bonnet before his nephew convinces him of the advisability of preserving an outward calm. Taking up the crown again, the Doge listens cautiously to the complaints of Israel Bertuccio—a plebeian unfairly assaulted by a nobleman; he learns of a plot to overthrow the Forty and reluctantly agrees to meet with the conspirators at

8. On Byron's departures from historical fact, see *PW*, IV, 326.

midnight. In Act II, Angiolina relates particulars of her life with the Doge (including her father's arrangement of the marriage), and characterizes Marino as a creature frequently disposed to intemperate displays of passion. Meanwhile, Bertuccio and Calendaro review their revolutionary plans: Calendaro doubts the determination of Bertram (another conspirator) where bloodshed may be required, but Bertuccio reassures him that all of their colleagues are trustworthy. While he awaits the arrival of Bertuccio at their point of rendezvous in Act III, Marino reflects upon his forebears as witnesses to his treachery against the state, but resolves to continue in his present course since he acts strictly in the cause of freedom. After the Doge is introduced to the conspirators, Bertram reiterates his earlier plea that some senators be spared but is soundly rebuked by his friends. Bertram's arguments momentarily weaken Marino's resolve, as he recalls his own former intimacy in military and political maneuvers with the present statesmen. Still, the cause of liberty triumphs, and Marino advises the conspirators to launch their attack at sunrise when St. Mark's bell tolls.

Act IV opens on Lioni, a patrician, as he contemplates the beauty and peacefulness of the evening, only to be interrupted by Bertram, who, in his eagerness to save the life of his friend, reveals the conspiratorial plot and is captured. Consequently, no sooner has the bell begun to peal than Marino and Bertuccio Faliero are arrested on charges of high treason. In Act V occurs the trial and sentencing of all the revolutionaries, including Marino, who is allowed a brief parting moment with Angiolina. Immediately before his execution, the Doge addresses the sun, reaffirms his innocence in the cause of freedom, and dies as the Venetian citizenry murmurs ominously against the injustice of the Forty.

So bare an outline hardly reveals the dramatic possibilities afforded the dramatist by the history of Marino Faliero, but Byron was fully aware of what might be done with the tale.[9] To John Murray's warning that he courted disadvantageous comparison with

---

9. Byron wrote extensively in his letters about *Marino Faliero*. Many of his remarks concern his adherence to historical fact, on which point he was annoyingly adamant; most of the rest defend his preservation of the three unities or the non-political purposes of the drama. See *L & J*, IV, 58–59; V, 51, 52, 62, 67, 84, 89–91, and 95–96.

Otway by dramatizing Venetian history, Byron retorted: "the story of Marino Falieri [sic] is different, and, I think, so much finer, that I wish Otway had taken it instead: the head conspiring against the body for refusal of redress for a real injury,—jealousy[10]—treason, with the more fixed and inveterate passions (mixed with policy) of an old and elderly man—the devil himself could not have a finer subject, and he is your only tragic dramatist."[11] This, possibly, is Byron's most articulate prose enunciation of a theme, which, in a variety of forms, figures prominently in almost all of his non-satiric poetry. Clashes of reason with passion, intellect with emotion, are by now commonplace; but in *Marino Faliero* Byron enriches his favorite motif by representing his protagonist as an eighty-year-old aristocrat flung into intellectual and emotional chaos by a conflict pitting personal against political values. Byron's early heroes wail tiresomely about having aged beyond their years; here we find a man old and settled enough to resist fiercely any challenge to established, "fixed and inveterate passions." But ironically, Marino Faliero, for all his ranting and occasionally empty attitudinizing, is better equipped to make decisions than most of Byron's former protagonists. Alterations of orthodox patterns of thought and conduct are for him insufferable; but his triumph of character resides in the apparent insurmountability of the intellectual and emotional barriers he must overcome.

To distinguish between the emotional and intellectual conflicts which beset Marino is almost impossible, for they fuse in his emergent realization that as a political figure he lacks power, and hence,

10. As Byron comments in the "Preface" to *Marino Faliero*, Matthew Lewis cautioned him against making the jealousy motif central: " 'If you make him jealous,' said he, 'recollect that you have to contend with established writers, to say nothing of Shakespeare, and an exhausted subject:—stick to the old fiery Doge's natural character, which will bear you out, if properly drawn.' " Byron followed this good advice; jealousy in Marino Faliero is nowhere apparent.

11. *L & J,* IV, 91–92 (2 April 1817). The temptation to quote an additional comment on Otway in the same letter is irresistible: "I am aware of what you say of Otway; and am a very great admirer of his,—all except of that maudlin bitch of chaste lewdness and blubbering curiosity, Belvidera, whom I utterly despise, abhor, and detest." Byron of course avoids any such representation of female passion in his characterizations of Angiolina *(Marino Faliero)* and Myrrah *(Sardanapalus).*

because his entire career has been devoted to statesmanship, as a man he is weak, ineffectual, and thoroughly dispensable. Marino's disillusionment (or, perhaps, awakening) is profoundly shattering, not only because his aristocratic pride and dignity are traduced, but also because he has betrayed his ancestry by permitting the leadership of Venice to slip from his control. Deeply rooted in the past, adamantly opposed to change, thrust into a position of responsibility he did not wish to accept, and now stripped of the rights of nobility and (to his view) of the respect due all noblemen, Marino demands a means by which he can reassert his fundamental worth as a human being and re-establish his competence as a leader of men. The real issue, then, is the conflict between Marino's religious respect for political and aristocratic tradition and his emotional desire to re-affirm his integrity as a human being, even though a violation of that tradition may be the sole means to do so. Marino must achieve a moral identity independent of the past, opposed to the depravity of the Forty, and correspondent with his vision of a cleansed, relatively democratic Venetian state.

Recurring throughout *Marino Faliero,* these four motifs—tradition, demoralization, revenge, and purgation—are supported by a complex pattern of imagery which at once strengthens their intellectual substance and intensifies their emotional impact. The larger outlines of the configurative design are clear enough. Marino's psychological development from aristocratic conservatism through halting equivocation to self-sacrificial humanitarianism, for example, may be traced in Byron's gradual substitution of light figures for images of darkness and half-light. Scurrilous metaphors from the reptilian kingdom join with images of contamination and putrescence to illustrate the necessity of purifying the Venetian republic. More particularly, the present degeneracy of Venice, represented in organic figures of diseased vegetation, contrasts with the moral integrity of Marino's ancestry, represented in rock and granite images. Finally, the pattern of blood imagery unites the four major themes by stressing, as the context demands, virtuous, defiled, shed, or purified blood. Within this encompassing design, subsidiary metaphorical patterns are of course manifest, but this should suffice to indicate the general construct and aesthetic of Byron's imagery in the play.

One other related issue, however, deserves attention here. If Marino has been deceived, or has deceived himself, about the significance of his office, he will inevitably, upon his awakening, distinguish between the long-maintained appearance and the recently revealed reality of his position. This distinction, coupled with the Doge's reverence for a tradition he presumed himself to be upholding and with his hate of the injustices administered by the Forty without his endorsement, elicits from him vituperation against the political puppet-show of which he has been the featured attraction. In fact, the disparity between the genuine and the pretended initially illuminates Marino to his own departure from tradition and to the deterioration of the Venetian republic. Hence, the Doge, inspecting the ducal bonnet, sneers at the meaninglessness of his office:

> Hollow bauble!
> Beset with all the thorns that line a crown,
> Without investing the insulted brow
> With the all-swaying majesty of Kings;
> Thou idle, gilded, and degraded toy,
> Let me resume thee as I would a vizor.[12]
>
> (I, ii, 259–264)

This early reference to the degradation of the ducal position in a figure suggesting a childish plaything, and the added implication that Marino the *Doge* is another thing entirely from Marino the *man,* introduces one of the primary figurative patterns of the drama. In the same scene, Marino cautions Israel Bertuccio against exaggerating the power of the Doge, "which is a pageant;" his cap and robes are "But lent to the poor puppet who must play / Its part with all its empire in this ermine." Angiolina claims that the Forty, themselves devoid of honor,

> seek its seeming
> As they would look out for an ornament
> Of which they feel the want . . . .
>
> (II, i, 70–72)

12. The *Oxford English Dictionary* defines the figurative meaning of "vizor" as "An outward appearance or show under which something different is hid; a mask or a disguise."

The conspirators, moreover, speak of Marino as "a mere puppet," their "apparent sovereign;" and, in justifying to them his part in the rebellion, Marino alludes to "this monster of a state, / This mockery of a government." Again, he sees himself as

> A thing of robes and trinkets, dizened out
> To sit in state as for a Sovereign's picture:
> . . . A tool—a fool—a puppet. . . .
> (III, ii, 188–189; 194)

At his arraignment Marino acidly spurns the "foul, outward, juggling show of justice" dispensed by the Forty. Informed that his picture in the portrait gallery of the Faliero's shall remain forever veiled, Marino, in a sharply ironic transvaluation of his thought processes, concludes:

> The veil which blackens o'er this blighted name,
> And hides, or seems to hide, these lineaments,
> Shall draw more gazers than the thousand portraits
> Which glitter round it in their pictured trappings—
> (V, i, 502–505)

Finally, returning to the figure which introduced his repeated distinctions between genuine and artificial powers, the Doge gratefully (and officially) relinquishes "That shining mockery, the ducal bauble . . . fatal ornament."

If we recall now that Marino resumed the crown in Act I knowing it to be merely a "vizor" obscuring the real man underneath an empty show of royalty, and if we notice in the "veil" passage Marino's assurance that genuine virtue will triumph over the oppressive darkness imposed by tyrants, we may legitimately conclude that the drama figures forth the gradual revelation of the Doge's true character—his emergence from stultifying artificiality into active responsibility and ennobling, self-sacrificing endeavor. Originally, Marino simply desired redress for personal insult; he slowly learns that individual causes are secondary to the fulfillment of a humanitarian good. His enthusiastic resignation from office signifies his awareness of the emptiness of that position, and reveals his belated recognition of the meaning of human dignity.

Correlative with this appearance-reality motif is Byron's use of light and dark imagery. The integration of light imagery, for example, with the appearance-reality theme is explicit in Lioni's soliloquy (IV, i, 23–111), in which the distinction between genuineness and artificiality is framed in a series of figurative contrasts. Returned from an evening's carouse with Venetian nobles, Lioni finds the moonlight and the night itself infinitely more satisfying than

> Those vast and dimly-latticed galleries,
> A dazzling mass of artificial light,
> Which showed all things, but nothing as they were.
>
> (IV, i, 32–34)

In the pale light of the ballroom, wrinkled Age trusted "the falsehood / Of the indulgent beams, which show, yet hide," and feared the sunrise which will stream "On sallow cheeks and sunken eyes." Lioni recalls "All the delusion of the dizzy scene, / Its false and true enchantments," the irregularity, the distortion, the indistinguishability of the real from the simulated, all because of the dim, artificial beams that suffused the scene. On the other hand, the moon (or natural light), ironically enough, relieves his bosom of a "cold heaviness," tranquilizes his anxious spirit, and, as he thinks, reveals everything as perfectly "congenial with the night." The passage is too lengthy to fit well into the drama, but its intoxicating lyricism offers a necessary relaxation of the tension steadily maintained through three acts; and it also demonstrates Byron's interest and effectiveness in employing variously an established image pattern.

The pattern is fixed early in *Marino Faliero*. As G. Wilson Knight remarks, the play takes place "mostly in half-light;" indeed, pale, cold moonlight dominates the atmosphere in almost every scene. Opening in late afternoon or early evening, *Marino Faliero* moves slowly toward the midnight rendezvous of the conspirators, pauses momentarily for Lioni's meditation, advances sluggishly toward dawn, and concludes, triumphantly though paradoxically, with Marino's execution amid a dazzling sunrise. Symbolizing political liberation for the state and personal redemption for the Doge, the dawn is both feared (because of the death it will bring to old friends) and joyously anticipated (because it will introduce freedom and justice into a politically and morally depraved republic). Sunlight, moreover, is linked figuratively with life, virtue, energy, and, by implication, order; while twilight, sunset, moonlight, and darkness are variously associated with death, corruption, chaos, and treachery. The moon, writes Knight, appears "not for romantic glamour, but rather for its steely pallor suiting the hard ethical precisions, cold vices, and chaste virtues of the somewhat grave conception."[13] Certainly, Byron's ethical delineations in works preceding this play seldom have the shading necessary for realistic presentation. He has few morally "gray" personae because he too frequently viewed human nature as either black or white. But the moon in *Marino Faliero* is used not so much to crystallize in an image the harsh precision of Byron's moral point of view as it is to present figuratively the ethical ambiguity of Marino's decision to join the conspirators. In the Third Canto of *Childe Harold's Pilgrimage,* Byron had represented Napoleon and Rousseau as now good, now wicked; but in this drama the poet's maturing insight is manifest in his characterization of Marino as noble and mean at the same time. Sunlight and darkness, then, are not, except in the broadest conception, antipodal images: they continually blur into each other, and the result is a sturdy metaphorical support for the ethical equivocation of Marino's thoughts, the moral ambiguity of his actions.

Before he learns of the conspiratorial plot, Marino's ethic is still uncomplicated by the necessity for moral choice between two diametrically opposed modes of conduct. Seeking reparation for personal inury, he can in good conscience counsel his nephew that black is black and white is white:

> Let it [our cause] be black among your dreams; and when
> The morn returns, so let it stand between
> The Sun and you, as an ill-omened cloud
> Upon a summer-day of festival . . . .
> (I, ii, 245–248)

Dawn at this point promises only dark remembrance of the besmirched Faliero name. But no sooner has Marino uttered his un-

13. "The Two Eternities: An Essay on Byron," in *The Burning Oracle* (New York: Oxford University Press, 1939), p. 235.

qualified pronouncement and mused in a soliloquy over the means by which he may requite the injustice, than he vaguely perceives the political and personal complications consequent upon any rash act against the omnipotent Forty. In the twilight, his former assurance shades into studied equivocation:

> as yet 'tis [my plan] but a chaos
> Of darkly brooding thoughts: my fancy is
> In her first work, more nearly to the light
> Holding the sleeping images of things
> For the selection of the pausing judgment.
> (I, ii, 282–286)

Yet, in Marino's variable psychological condition, the gentle prodding of Israel Bertuccio convinces him, at least momentarily, that the conspirators' goal is the political liberation of Venice. Not altogether assured that his proposed behavior can be differentiated from Steno's (who groveled "by stealth in the moon's glimmering light"), Marino, nevertheless, in a passage foreshadowing the significant role of light in the play's concluding scenes, compares honorable action to the sun:

> Virtue
> Stands like the Sun, and all which rolls around
> Drinks life, and light, and glory from her aspect.
> (II, i, 396–398)

His former dread of the dawn has only slightly, and temporarily, diminished, but Marino determines upon a form of revenge for his calumniators and interprets the fulfillment of that revenge as a symbolic "dawn" even in his old age. Rendered vengeance will provide a "mellowing" to "the last hours as the night [i.e., his death] approaches."

Byron adds yet another dimension to this pattern of light and dark imagery by fixing the rendezvous of Marino and Israel Bertuccio beneath an equestrian monument erected to the noble Faliero line. Acutely conscious of his departure from Faliero tradition, Marino thrice points to the "warrior's statue . . . in the dim light / Of the dull moon" as a defense against Bertuccio's insidious arguments. Far from insensible to the meaning of the treachery upon which he is about to embark, Marino is caught in this twilight of indecisiveness, fearing on the one hand the darkness of the conspiratorial meeting, and yearning, on the other, for the sunrise of political and individual restoration. The wash of the moonlight epitomizes in an image the equivocal state of Marino's mind.

Perhaps this is the place to examine more closely the rationale behind the Doge's casuistry and the moral complexity of the entire drama. I have noted above various motifs connected respectively with sunlight and darkness; but the symbolic importance of moonlight remains obscure until we understand that each value linked to the sun implies its opposite, associated with darkness. The rehabilitation of life in the political and personal senses, for example, necessitates the death of an obsolete system and many of its partisans. The establishment of virtue as the controlling principle of life requires the employment of deceptive tactics which (to Marino) seem more befitting for traitors than for heroes. The creation of order implies the destruction of a semblance of order, peacefully preserved in Venice for ages, and the introduction of temporary chaos. Finally, a free life for Venetians may be secured only by devious means. Any impulse toward precipitate action in Marino is strongly mollified by his awareness of what is politically and morally at stake. Much of the play, then, does occur in half-light—the shadowy moonlight of Marino's incertitude.

From the moment of his unanimous election as leader of the rebellion, Marino sees in the anticipated sunrise the promise of political freedom and personal redemption. Consequently, metaphors of darkness and moonlight are replaced by figures of either the real or the expected dawn. The Doge promises that a "dawn of mercy" will follow this "last night of mere words;" the expurgation of Venice will ensue

> In the absorbing, sweeping, whole revenge,
> Which, like the sheeted fire from Heaven, must blast
> Without distinction, as it fell of yore,
> Where the Dead Sea hath quenched two Cities' ashes.
>   (III, ii, 420–423)

Marino repeatedly inquires after the progress of the night, and trembling with anticipation, he cries, "Will morn never put to rest / These stars which twinkle yet o'er all the heavens?" Detecting the first streaks of gray in the East, the Doge invokes the dawn:

> Thou Day!
> That slowly walk'st the waters! march—march on—
> I would not smite i' the dark . . . .
>
> (IV, ii, 138–140)

Dispatching his nephew to toll St. Mark's bell and launch the attack, Marino muses momentarily on the "blackness" of the day, but reassures himself that it "Shall be followed by a bright millennium." To the Signor of the Night who arrests him, the Doge remarks, "learn (if souls so much obscured can bear / To gaze upon the sunbeams) to be free." Disappointed but unbroken by the failure of the conspiracy, Marino dies with the sun's rays full upon him and the ominous murmurs of the Venetian public loud in his ears. My point is that with the fading of the moonlight and night figures in the drama, and with the increase of dawn and sunlight images, occurs a correspondent diminution of Marino's initial fear and a gradual stabilization of his commitment to the rebellion. Progressing from the original darkness of personal hate and ennui, through the moonlight of hesitation and equivocation, into the sunlight of determination and self-sacrificing action, Marino attains something very near messianic stature: at least his dignity as a human being is reaffirmed and the eventual liberation of his people is a possibility. Throughout the tragedy, then, the interplay of light and dark imagery functions both as a complement to the theme of freedom and as an index to the development of Marino's mind.

The necessity for purging the Venetian state issues most emphatically through an abundance of reptilian and animal images and a variety of corresponding figures of foulness, taintedness, and corruption. Himself "stung at the heart," Marino, for example, retains nothing but virulence for Steno, "this creeping, coward, rank, acquitted felon, / Who threw his sting into a poisonous libel;" the Venetian republic is an

> o'er grown aristocratic Hydra,
> The poisonous heads of whose envenomed body
> Have breathed a pestilence upon us all.
>
> (I, ii, 421–423)

Again, Venice is a "scorpion nest of vice;" and "the blighting venom" of Steno's "sweltering heart . . . shall spread itself in general poison." Israel Bertuccio, embarrassed by his former desire to seek restitution against Barbaro for an individual grievance (a desire paralleling Marino's thirst for revenge against Steno), counsels himself that to place personal vengeance above the common good is to leave "one scorpion crushed, and thousands stinging." Countering Bertram's arguments that age and quality in some senators warrant pity from the conspirators, Calendaro retorts:

> Yes, such pity
> As when the viper hath been cut to pieces,
> The separate fragments quivering in the sun,
> In the last energy of venomous life,
> Deserve and have. Why, I should think as soon
> Of pitying some particular fang which made
> One in the jaw of the swoln serpent, as
> Of saving one of these . . . .
>
> (III, ii, 26–33)

Similarly, Angiolina, answering Steno's request for forgiveness, declaims:

> Pardon is for men,
> And not for reptiles—we have none for Steno,
> And no resentment: things like him must sting,
> And higher beings suffer: 'tis the charter
> Of Life. The man who dies by the adder's fang
> May have the crawler crushed, but feel no anger:
> 'Twas the worm's nature; and some men are worms
> In soul, more than the living things of tombs.
>
> (V, i, 458–465)

Now the poisonous or destructive element present in most of these images appears also in frequent figures of foulness and infection. The word "taint" occurs ten times in the play, "foul" nine times, and "vile" eight—each of the three often combined with references to plague, pestilence, and infection. Steno's affront was "the foulest stain" against the honor of the royal family, which was "tainted by the accusing breath / Of calumny and scorn." Marino, in an oblique allusion to the Forty, claims that he is not "Infected with that leprosy . . . Which taints the hoariest years of vicious men." Indeed, the Forty are afflicted with "rank hearts" and "infected blood;" Venice is "A lazar-house of tyranny" diseased by the "patrician pestilence." Lurking in "The present institutions of Venice," the Doge believes, is a "fatal poison to the springs of life;" that fact he knows from experience: "I had one only fount of quiet left, / And that they poisoned." Or again: "My very hearth was stained / By the pollution of your ribaldry." His single purpose, Marino vows, is "To spill / The rank polluted current from the veins / Of a few bloated despots." And in a venomous repudiation of Venice's present corruption, the Doge deems it a "den of drunkards with the blood of princes! / Gehenna of the waters! Thou sea Sodom!"

Two obvious facts about these figures of reptilian life and defiled human character must be conceded: they are excessively repetitive, particularly in their use of adjectives, and there is nothing especially subtle about Byron's use of them to fortify his themes of corruption and purgation. On the other hand, however, I would remark that these images bear most of the weight of emotional communication; and because of their repetition we sense the terrible pain of Marino's burden and the unavoidable necessity for his participation in the rebellion. With such an inveterate belief in the honor of and due his office, Marino is bound to interpret any offense against the ducal crown as the result of man's basest animal impulses; and he is bound also to phrase his complaints in the most abusive language at his disposal. The reptilian imagery and the scurrilous figures of foulness and infection, then, are perfectly appropriate to the Doge's outrage over the defamation of his position, to the character of the offenders, and to Marino's compelling urge for revenge.

A substantial part of Marino's appetite for vengeance is rooted in guilt over having betrayed his ancestral heritage. His tie with an abstract tradition and his personal devotion both to his own and to

Angiolina's father render his proposed break with an inherited cus-
tom of belief and conduct severely trying. And once again, Byron's
imagery reinforces a theme: the honor of Marino's forebears and his
hope of re-establishing a respectable republic are cast in rock or
granite imagery, and the present demoralization of Venice, and of his
own character, are described in organic figures. Hence, Dagolino
advises the conspirators,

> The spirit of this Aristocracy
>   . . . must be rooted out; and if there were
> A single shoot of the old tree in life,
> 'Twould fasten in the soil, and spring again
> To gloomy verdure and to bitter fruit.
>   (III, ii, 40–44)

Anticipating the slaughter with unaccustomed relish, the Doge pre-
dicts that the Council "Will then be gathered in unto the harvest, /
And we will reap them with the sword for sickle." On his own loss of
power, Marino reflects that his friends

>   fell from me
> As faithless leaves drop from the o'erblown flower,
> And left me a lone blighted thorny stalk,
> Which, in its solitude, can shelter nothing;
> So, as they let me wither, let them perish!
>   (III, ii, 308–312)

Finally, he reiterates his determination to

>   strike the blow,
> Which shall unpeople many palaces,
> And hew the highest genealogic trees
> Down to the earth, strewed with their bleeding fruit,
> And crush their blossoms into barrenness.
>   (III, ii, 491–495)

Contrasting to these figures of decaying vegetation are configurations suggesting the structural stability of genuine honor. Distraught
over the leniency of the Forty and undetermined of his course of
action, Marino locates no virtue on earth save in "the rock / Of
faith connubial;" even "An incarnation of the poet's god / In all his

marble-chiselled beauty," Marino alleges in a figure paradoxically prescient of his identification of true honor with the statue of his sire, "Would not suffice to bind where virtue is not." Act III opens on the Doge reverent before the "Tall fane" erected to the memory of his ancestors, in which he sees represented the unsullied honor and scrupulous nobility which characterized their tenures of office. To Israel Bertuccio, who observes only "a tall warrior's stature / Bestriding a proud steed," the Doge warns that there is "a spirit / In such things;" and he constantly feels the need to justify his conduct to his sires' ghosts. Foreseeing the renewal of "times of truth and justice," Marino determines to condense

> in a fair free commonwealth
> Not rash equality but equal rights,
> Proportioned like the columns to the temple,
> Giving and taking strength reciprocal,
> And making firm the whole with grace and beauty,
> So that no part could be removed without
> Infringement of the general symmetry.
> (III, ii, 169–175)

Finally, in proof of her own invulnerability and high-minded honor, Angiolina claims that to her "the scorner's words were as the wind / Unto the rock."[14]

This should be sufficient evidence to indicate Byron's thematic use of these organic and rock figures. He employs the organic metaphors not only to show that the aristocracy has grown "from the soil of its

14. It is possible to see Angiolina as another of Byron's counterpart figures, although her performance in that role is considerably less striking than that of Byron's earlier and later women. Where Marino tends to be merciless and reckless, Angiolina is compassionate and calm; where he vacillates, she remains firm; where he can find only evil in his contemporaries, she seeks to instill in him the Christian virtue of her father:

> subdue all tendency to lend
> The best and purest feeling of our nature
> To baser passions.
> (II, i, 96–98)

Angiolina addresses these lines to her maid, but they epitomize the instructions she consistently offers Marino. Knight sees her as "a personification of uncompromising Christian idealism" (p. 240).

own past,"[15] but also to emphasize the capacity for decay and disintegration (or growth and continuity) that any living community possesses. As an aristocrat, Marino the Doge is as responsible as any for the present state of political depravity: his duty, therefore, is to dig out the rotten roots of Venetian government and set about recultivating the garden. The norm by which his conduct will be judged is the moral integrity—imaged in rock figures—preserved by his ancestry. But Marino does not deceive himself that any society can at once live and maintain a statuesque quality. The social and political order which the Doge envisages is quite subtly "conceived not precisely as a living organism but, being still a dream in the mind only, as a work of art, a temple."[16] That is, a social combine may be founded upon a concept of sturdy, rock-like honor, but by no means can it survive statically.

One additional—and perhaps the most important—image pattern remains for consideration: *Marino Faliero* is from first to last bathed in a metaphorical sea of blood. The significance of the references to blood lies not so much in their frequency as in the fact that the major themes of tradition (or honor), corruption, revenge, and purgation all are presented, respectively, in figures of noble, polluted, spilled, and cleansed blood. Hence, the pattern of blood imagery may be viewed as the metaphorical norm for the drama, the function of which is to combine imagistically the four primary themes and to provide a point of departure for further figurative explorations by the poet within the limits of their own thematic frameworks. A few examples may clarify my meaning. Speaking of his devotion to the honor and tradition of the Venetian state, Marino assures Israel Bertuccio that

> not for any knot of men,
> Nor sect, nor faction, did I bleed or sweat!
> But would you know why I have done all this?
> Ask of the bleeding pelican why she
> Hath ripped her bosom? Had the bird a voice,
> She'd tell thee 'twas for *all* her little ones.
>
> (I, ii, 438–443)

15. Knight, p. 230.
16. *Ibid.*, p. 233.

The Doge remarks repeatedly about "the blood and sweat of almost eighty years," the "noble," "bold," and "pure high blood" of his sires, the "blood of Loredano [Angiolina's father] / Pure in your veins," the "alliances of blood and marriage," his own "friends by blood," and his dedication to the Venetian republic "which I have bled for, and the foreign earth, / Which drank this willing blood from many a wound." But in contrast to such purity and self-sacrifice, the present depravity of Venice is represented in the "infected blood" of her noblemen. Israel Bertuccio bears upon his face the blood which signifies the corruption of the Senate, and he fears the moment when the senators may again "wring blood" from him. Calendaro is apprehensive that Bertram may "Turn sick at sight of blood, although a villain's." And Marino vows to spill "The rank polluted current from the veins / Of a few bloated despots;" after all, he inquires,

> What
> Are a few drops of human blood? 'tis false,
> The blood of tyrants is not human . . . .
> (IV, ii, 161–163)

Furthermore, the desire for revenge and the necessity for purgation are played off against each other in a series of blood figures. On the one hand Marino feels justified in seeking personal revenge, but he occasionally balks at the need for slaughtering former comrades; and on the other hand he is convinced that general massacre is the only means to total purgation. Israel Bertuccio's advice to Calendaro on the nature of revenge foreshadows his later argument to the Doge:

> these same drops of blood,
> Shed shamefully, shall have the whole of his [Barbaro's]
> For their requital—But not only his;
> We will not strike for private wrongs alone:
> Such are for selfish passions and rash men.
> (II, ii, 11–15)

But Marino is difficult to convince. The sight of blood "which spouts through hoary scalps," he says, is not "To me a thing of triumph." Outraged at Israel's apparent heartlessness and fearing his own hesitation, Marino exclaims:

> You *feel* not—*you* go to this butcher-work
> As if these high-born men were steers for shambles:
> When all is over, you'll be free and merry,
> And calmly wash those hands incarnadine.
>   (III, ii, 506–509)

Left alone just before dawn, the Doge, no longer hesitating, does feel a final pang of remorse; he addresses the ocean:

> Now thou must wear an unmixed crimson; no
> Barbaric blood can reconcile us now
> Unto that horrible incarnadine,
> But friend or foe will roll in civic slaughter.
>   (IV, ii, 145–148)

Against these emotions of regret and fear should be placed Marino's conviction that bloodshed is justified, first because sanctioned by the laws of heaven and mankind, and second because it may cleanse the state. Early in the drama, the Doge's conception of revenge is simplistic and naive: "Does not the law of Heaven say blood for blood?" he asks. "Do not the laws of man say blood for honor? . . . Say not the laws of nations blood for treason?" But very gradually and very subtly this Hebraic notion shades into the concept of blood as purger. Contemporary Venice is to Marino a "spectre / Which must be exorcised with blood." Israel Bertuccio is willing to shed his own blood so that it might flow "between the murderers and the murdered, washing / The prison and the palace walls." And Marino vows to "wash away / The plague spots in the healing wave," "to cleanse the commonwealth." Finally, Israel, conceding that the cleansing of Venice has failed, feels secure in the knowledge that the conspirators have saved themselves—preserved their own honor and fulfilled their responsibilities—by instigating the rebellion:

> So shall our blood more readily arise
> To Heaven against them, and more testify
> To their atrocities . . . .
>   (V, i, 118–120)

The Doge echoes the same sentiment: "my blood will rise / To Heaven before the souls of those who shed it." Although the attempts by the plotters to cleanse the body politic have failed, at least for the moment, Marino and the rest have dissociated themselves from the degradation of the state, have, in fact, purged themselves of the "taint" to which, as subjects of the Forty, they were heirs. Above all, Marino has reaffirmed the nobility of his own blood by sacrificing it to Venetian honor.

I I

While the setting and characters of *Sardanapalus*[17] are vastly different from those of *Marino Faliero,* various image patterns in the later tragedy assume a function of even greater importance for this discussion. A brief review of the plot of *Sardanapalus* may clear the way for an examination of its imagery.

Salemenes, brother-in-law of Sardanapalus, King of Assyria, interrupts his sovereign's plans for a midnight banquet on the banks of the Euphrates with the news that a large-scale rebellion threatens the kingdom. The effeminate king, incredulous at such a notion and chagrined at Salemenes' insistence that the revels be held indoors, reluctantly consigns his signet to his brother-in-law, thereby empowering him with the royal authority to quell the revolt. At the urging of Myrrah, Sardanapalus' Greek consort, the king agrees to remain within the palace for the evening's festivities. In Act II, Salemenes attempts to arrest the two chief conspirators (Beleses, a priest, and Arbaces), but Arbaces resists, a brawl ensues, Sardanapalus subdues the participants, and, to Salemenes' despair, temporarily excuses

17. On Byron's historical accuracy in *Sardanapalus,* see *PW,* V, 4–5: "Byron's Sardanapalus, with his sudden transition from voluptuous abandonment to heroic chivalry, his remorseful recognition of the sanctities of wedlock, his general good nature, his 'sly, insinuating sarcasms' (Moore's Diary, Sept. 30, 1821, *Memoirs,* iii, 282), 'all made out of the carver's brain,' resembles *history* as little as *history* resembles the Assyrian record. Fortunately, the genius of the poet escaped from the meshes which he had woven round himself, and, in spite of himself, he was constrained to 'beat his music out,' regardless of his authorities." Cf. Byron's claims in his "Preface" to the tragedy: "it has been my intention to follow the account of Diodorus Siculus; reducing it, however, to such dramatic regularity as I best could, and trying to approach the unities." See also the discussion of Samuel C. Chew, *The Dramas of Lord Byron* (New York: Russell and Russell, 1964 [reissued]), pp. 103ff.

both Beleses and Arbaces. Later, however, under pressure from Salemenes, the king exiles both schemers to their satrapies.

The banquet is no sooner under way in Act III than Pania, Sardanapalus' trusted officer, arrives, wounded, with news that fighting
between the king's troops and the conspirators has broken out within
the city's gates. The king immediately calls for his armor, defends
himself admirably against Beleses, receives a slight wound in the
battle, but for the moment forces his enemies into a retreat. In Act
IV, Sardanapalus recounts to Myrrah a horrible nightmare in which
two of his ancestors, Nimrod and Semiramis, subjected him to unut-
terable terrors. He is then temporarily "unmanned" by an interview
with the queen, Zarina, and his sons, but arranges for their escape
and launches yet another attack. The second assault proves fatal for
Salemenes (Act V), who is thus spared the information that the
flooding river has opened the city's walls to the traitors, and that
Ofrantes (Salemenes' dearest friend) and his troops have defected to
Beleses. Knowing that further resistance is futile, Sardanapalus refuses Beleses' terms of surrender but pardons his messenger, commits
his treasure to Pania, orders him to follow Zarina, surrounds the
throne with fagots, and dies with Myrrah amid the flames.

The conflicting tendencies of Sardanapalus' mind are emphasized
through four acts of the tragedy in images of "bisexuality"[18]—that
is, figures simultaneously suggesting both the masculine and feminine
features of the king's character. The feminine element dominates at
the outset, but Salemenes recognizes the hermaphroditic nature of his
sovereign:

> In his effeminate heart
> There is a careless courage which Corruption
> Has not all quenched, and latent energies,
> Repressed by circumstance, but not destroyed—
> Steeped, but not drowned, in deep voluptuousness.
>   (I, i, 9–13)

Sardanapalus, "the man-queen," appears "amidst the damsels, / As

18. "The hero, poet-like, is somewhat bisexual, aiming to fuse man's reason
with woman's emotional depth, whilst repudiating the evil concomitants"
(Knight, p. 247).

femininely garbed, and scarce less female;" Salemenes is inclined to classify Sardanapalus as one of the "beings less than women" who populate the king's entourage. To the conspirators he is a "she-king," "less than woman," a whining "silkworm," a "she-Sardanapalus." Perhaps the most effective visual representation of the king's bisexuality occurs when, after donning his armor, he preens himself before a mirror:[19]

> This cuirass fits me well, the baldric better,
> And the helm not at all. Methinks I seem
> Passing well in these toys . . . .
> (III, i, 163–165)

From this point on, however, the feminine element diminishes, and is replaced (1) by Sardanapalus' self-counsel against yielding to effeminate indulgences and (2) by the remarks of other characters on the unexpected alteration of his character. Comparing her lord to Alcides, Myrrah sees him now as a new Hercules, who, though "Nursed in effeminate arts from youth to manhood," and though rushing into battle "As though it were a bed of love," deserves all the honor and admiration of any Greek hero. Sardanapalus does not wish to see his sons, lest the encounter "Unman my heart;" "I grow womanish again, and must not," he advises himself: "I must learn sternness now. My sins have all / Been of the softer order." Pondering those sins near the end of Act IV, he philosophizes painfully, but realistically,

> To what gulfs
> A single deviation from the track
> Of human duties leads even those who claim
> The homage of mankind as their born due.
> (IV, i, 432–435)

Finally, after verifying his manhood through spirited participation in military engagements, Sardanapalus asserts neither his militancy nor

---

19. Cf. Byron's letter to Murray, 30 May 1821: "In the third act, when Sardanapalus calls for a *mirror* to look at himself in his *armour,* recollect to quote the Latin passage from *Juvenal* upon *Otho* (a similar character, who did the same thing [*Satire,* ii, ll. 99–103]): Gifford will help you to it. The trait is perhaps too familiar, but it is historical (of *Otho,* at least,) and natural in an effeminate character" (*L & J,* V, 301).

his epicureanism, but rather his humanity: "I am not a soldier but a man." The tragedy, then, dramatizes the fusion of the king's equally strong masculine and feminine impulses: whereas an effeminate emotionalism dominates his mental and physical activities at the opening of the drama, a rigorous intellectualism and combativeness determine his actions through the middle section, only to evolve at the denouement into a philosophy of compassionate humanism. Through his use of these images of bisexuality, Byron quite subtly presents at once the dualism of Sardanapalus' character and prepares, from the outset of the drama, for the ultimate union of the two principles in his hero. The struggle for supremacy between the masculine and feminine proclivities of the king, of course, forms the crux of his mental torment, and the reconciliation of these antipodal impulses is not so easily accomplished as my short quotations may indicate. The mere introduction of a military conflict is an insufficient impetus to activate Sardanapalus' faltering masculinity; nor is he the only character in the drama distinguished by a degree of bisexuality. Various forces exert strong influences upon him; and among them, Myrrah and Salemenes are the most significant.

Myrrah, as a matter of fact, functions, as the specific occasion demands, as a male or female counterpart to the female or male Sardanapalus: she consistently represents through four acts the state of emotional and intellectual maturity which the king must attain. Aware of her function, she vows in Act I to "teach him how to reign." Myrrah, it may be remarked, also represents a considerable advance over the earlier Astarte figure in *Manfred,* for her performance as counterpart here is both active and salutary: where her sovereign is weak and negligent, she is strong and industrious; where he is foolish and self-indulgent, she is wise and restrained; where he is indecisive and peevish, she is resolute and altruistic. Appropriately enough, as Sardanapalus moves closer toward the reconciliation of his masculine with his feminine impulses, Myrrah's role as "masculine" counterpart diminishes in importance, and the Greek slave assumes her proper place as a subservient, deeply affectionate companion to the king.[20]

20. Two of Byron's remarks on the love element in the drama are illuminating. A journal entry of 13 January 1821 includes the following comment: "[Teresa Guiccioli] quarreled with me, because I said that love was *not the loftiest* theme for true tragedy; and, having the advantage of her native

The spiritual affinity between Sardanapalus and Myrrah is explicit from the beginning of the play; the king believes

> that some unknown influence, some sweet oracle,
> Communicates between us, though unseen
> In absence, and attracts us to each other.
>
> (I, ii, 424–427)

All of Salemenes' counsel about the seriousness of the conspiracy produces little visible effect on Sardanapalus, but the "sanguinary" Myrrah, sensing the gravity of the situation, convinces her sovereign of the necessity for circumspect conduct. Salemenes discerns in Myrrah the single hope of saving the king:

> Let him not sink back into luxury.
> You have more power upon his spirit than
> Wisdom within these walls, or fierce rebellion
> Raging without: look well that he relapse not.
>
> (III, i, 416–419)

Fearful lest such a relapse occur, and slightly unsettled by Sardanapalus' vain primping before the mirror, Myrrah accompanies him into battle, and to the king's astonished delight, proves herself every bit his equal, if not his superior. She was, Sardanapalus relates,

> like the dam
> Of the young lion, femininely raging
> (And femininely meaneth furiously,
> Because all passions in excess are female),
> Against the hunter flying with her cub,

language, and natural female eloquence, she overcame my fewer arguments. I believe she was right. I must put more love into *Sardanapalus* than I intended" (*L & J,* V, 173). And, to John Murray on 4 July 1821, he wrote: "as I think that *love* is not the principal passion for tragedy (and yet most of ours turn upon it), you will not find me a popular writer. Unless it is Love, *furious, criminal,* and *hapless,* it ought not to make a tragic subject: when it is melting and maudlin, it *does,* but it ought not to do" (*L & J,* V, 218). Byron had completed the tragedy in May, and looking back upon it, he accurately described the kind of love represented in Sardanapalus' relationships with Myrrah and Zarina. But it is worth noting that he seems not to have intended love as the central passion; the crux of the drama is the king's growth from voluptuous, self-indulgent passivity to stern, courageous, and self-abnegating action.

> She urged on with her voice and gesture, and
> Her floating hair and flashing eyes, the soldiers
> In the pursuit.
>
> (III, i, 378–385)

Not improbably, Myrrah's warrior-like conduct spurred not only the troops, but Sardanapalus himself to at least temporary conquest of the conspirators. Moreover, the parenthetical statement in this quotation is significant for its revelation of the king's progress toward emotional and intellectual balance. For the first time he admits, although obliquely, the dangers consequent upon indiscriminately indulged passions. Myrrah, of course, was not at fault in her passionate excess; but Sardanapalus, perhaps unconsciously, senses the dangers of intemperance in his own character. At any rate, Myrrah's strength, courage, and resolution are in large measure responsible for the king's final spiritual triumph, and the Greek minion is rewarded for her efforts with the assurance that her union with Sardanapalus is sanctified and immortalized by the "commingling fire":

> pure as is my love to thee, shall they [our ashes],
> Purged from the dross of earth, and earthly passion,
> Mix pale with thine.
>
> (V, i, 472–474)

For political and personal reasons, a legal alliance between Sardanapalus and Myrrah was impossible during their lifetimes, but in a kind of symbolic marriage by fire, the king is eternally joined in death with his female counterpart, to whom belongs much of the credit for his psychological victory.

Three other characters, however, may claim a share in Sardanapalus' conquest over the tyrannous femininity of his being—Salemenes, Semiramis, and Nimrod, all of whom function to some degree as counterpart figures. The personality of the austere, "cool, stern Salemenes" is in every respect directly opposed to that of the king, as Sardanapalus himself is aware. Recognizing his brother-in-law's administrative and military abilities, the king says to him, "You should have been monarch," and symbolically surrenders sovereignty of Assyria by placing the king's signet on Salemenes' finger. But Salemenes is as immoderate in his crusade against Beleses and Arbaces as Sardanapalus is in his evening revels: when the king demands that justice be tempered with mercy, Salemenes relinquishes the ring, and the fate of Assyria rests again with Sardanapalus. Nevertheless, up to a point, Salemenes embodies the strong-willed masculinity which has for so long remained latent in the king. Sardanapalus perceives the difference between them:

> That man is of a temper too severe;
> Hard but lofty as the rock, and free
> From all the taints of common earth—while I
> Am softer clay, impregnated with flowers.
> (II, i, 519–522)

The comparison is ultimately beneficial, for it leads Sardanapalus to bitter regret over his physical and temperamental flaccidity, and hence stimulates him to pattern his conduct after that of his brother-in-law. After Salemenes' death, Sardanapalus' gratitude to him for reawakening dormant manliness is properly reflected in his treatment of the body: he instructs that the corpse be borne to

> my proper chamber.
> Place it beneath my canopy, as though
> The King lay there . . . .
> (V, i, 164–166)

As the king's "brother" (Sardanapalus frequently refers to Salemenes as such), therefore, Salemenes personifies the stern masculinity which Sardanapalus must incorporate into his character; when the king ultimately reaches that goal, Salemenes becomes dispensable. But as an efficacious counterpart to the king, Salemenes and his services are quite as essential as those of Myrrah.

Of lesser significance as counterpart figures are Semiramis and Nimrod, founders of the Assyrian empire and ancestors of Sardanapalus. Semiramis, though a woman,[21] was Assyria's greatest warrior,

---

21. Whereas Sardanapalus is more woman than man at the outset of the drama, Semiramis is the exact opposite:

> —a woman only—led
> These our Assyrians to the solar shores
> of Ganges,
> and returned
> like a *man*—a hero . . . .
> (I, ii, 173–176)

and Nimrod lived primarily, so the drama intimates, for the pleasure of the hunt: but both of them embody a cruel animal instinct, an inhuman bestiality, the remnants of which may be observed in Sardanapalus' voluptuousness. Whereas they thirsted respectively for the blood of men and beasts, Sardanapalus is too frequently inclined to indulge his animal sexual passion; and it is that same bestial instinct which causes the king to rush to battle as though it were "a bed of love." Knight points out that Semiramis and Nimrod "represent all traditional values, and suggest the dark ingrained fear of ancestral authority whose weight so often masquerades as conscience."[22] True enough; for once Salemenes has reminded Sardanapalus of his departure from Assyrian military tradition, the king broods excessively upon the conquests of Semiramis and attempts to rationalize his own preservation of peace. Such brooding, of course, prompts the king's nightmare in Act IV, where the symbolic emphasis is on random and needless bloodshed, sadistic savagery, and the unprincipled exercise of power.[23] This dream, coming between the first and second assaults on the traitors, reveals to the king the dangers of unrestrained slaughter, prepares for his merciful pardon of Beleses' messenger, and distinguishes Nimrod and Semiramis as complements to the bestial side of Sardanapalus' character: by their examples the king learns, in part, to repress his own impulsive passions. Myrrah, Salemenes, Nimrod, and Semiramis, then, all contain within themselves conflicting penchants of the king's character, and as Sardanapalus gradually becomes aware of the dualism of his own nature, reflected in these counterparts, he can discriminate between the good and evil qualities of his own character.

Moreover, the evolution of Sardanapalus' psychological stability and his progress toward spiritual triumph are represented throughout the drama in images of light and darkness. Calling Murray's attention to the preservation of classical structure in *Sardanapalus,* Byron wrote: "You will remark that the *Unities* are all *strictly* observed. The time, a

22. P. 254.
23. Also in the dream sequence appears a strong suggestion of incestuous passion; the point of it is obscure unless it is intended as another example of bestial wantonness. Knight interprets the incestuous animalistic caresses of Semiramis as an imagistic opposite to the "pure sexual passions" of Myrrah (p. 254).

Summer's night, about nine hours, or less, though it begins before Sunset and ends after Sunrise."[24] By fixing the time-span of his tragedy between twilight and mid-morning, Byron probably had in mind more than the rules of Greek or Italian dramatic art. Light appears from several sources and in a variety of shades, integrates seemingly disparate themes, and illuminates both the debauchery and the ultimate victory of the king. Light imagery is related variously to the motifs of love, sensualism, war, religious orthodoxy and paganism, historical tradition, and, most importantly, to Sardanapalus' spiritual development. But the incoherence which might seem consequent upon so many and paradoxical uses of light is easily clarified by the particularization of sun, star, and fire imagery to support the theme of the disparity between man's desires and his limitations. This familiar Byronic motif weaves through the tragedy, supplying motivation for actions and credibility to characters, and endowing the play with a more universal meaning than that contained in Sardanapalus' individual triumph. Foreshadowing the primary conflict in his next tragedy, *Cain,* Byron contrasts in *Sardanapalus* the eternality, the omnipotence, and the magnificence of divine creatures with the impermanence, the ignorance, and the pettiness of mortal life. Deities, whether conventional or unorthodox, whether commanding a character's respect or scorn, are consistently figured in light images; and Byron even suggests that in Sardanapalus' concluding association with fire, the king has in death assumed a divine quality.

But the distance of the monarch's journey to divinity is explicit from the play's opening. Gods, priests, orthodox worship, religion of any sort are alien to his nature:

> I feel a thousand mortal things about me,
> But nothing god-like,—unless it may be
> The thing which you condemn, a disposition
> To love and to be merciful, to pardon
> The follies of my species, and (that's human)
> To be indulgent to my own.
>
> (I, ii, 273–278)

He frivolously jockeys with Salemenes over the relative merits of

24. *L & J,* V, 301 (30 May 1821).

Baal and Bacchus, and he drinks to the latter's title to greatness, "the immortal grape." With his tittering entourage of courtiers, Sardanapalus anticipates the forthcoming revels: "we shall gather like the stars above us, / And you will form a heaven as bright as theirs." Of Baal he will admit only that "thou shinest like a god." All eagerness for the "intoxicating glare" of the feast, he orders that the galley

> blaze with beauty and with light, until
> It seems unto the stars which are above us
> Itself an opposite star . . . .
>
> (I, ii, 556–558)

Later, he gloats over the sumptuousness of the banquet, claiming that it "Is my true realm, amidst bright eyes and faces," for "where the King is, pleasure sparkles."[25] Now we have in these lines a paradoxical presentiment of Sardanapalus' metaphorical connection with the sun and fire in Act V, for here, dissociated from religious orthodoxy, he intends to make of his pavilion a sort of paradisiacal haven, which will in its scintillating brilliance challenge the heavens themselves. The king's philosophy, expressed to Salemenes, is "Eat, drink, and love; the rest's not worth a fillip;" and he obviously considers himself a second Bacchus presiding over his revels, ablaze with lasciviousness of every variety. Notice, however, that the pavilion is illuminated with artificial light, and that Sardanapalus seems singularly determined to extinguish the natural light of the stars in the dazzle of his lamps.

Within the framework of light imagery, Byron provides a smooth transition from emphasis on starlight to concentration on sunlight, and thence to stress upon the godlike quality of the sun, in Beleses' long apostrophe to "thou true sun" opening Act II (ll. 1–36). As the "worshipper," "priest," and "servant" of Baal, Beleses naturally identifies the sun with his god, but he is curiously pessimistic, if not despairing, in his address to the deity. He sees in the crimson sunset a portent of bloodshed; but even so, the sun to him is "the burning

25. These two quotations appear after the initial sobering period when Sardanapalus glimpses momentarily the perilous condition of his reign, but they represent the same sort of reckless joviality and sensual indulgence—imaged in light figures—found in I, ii.

oracle of all that live," the "fountain of all life," and the everlasting symbol of him who bestows life. Still, as an astrologer he is baffled and as a man he is intimidated by the limitation of the sun's "lore" to calamitous events:

> Why not
> Unfold the rise of days more worthy thine
> All-glorious burst from ocean? why not dart
> A beam of hope athwart the future years,
> As of wrath to its days?
>
> (II, i, 18–22)

The real reason for Beleses' despondency, however, appears in the final lines of his soliloquy: the sun disappears, "and leaves his beauty, not his knowledge." The resplendent hues in the sun's wake lead Beleses to muse,

> Yet what is
> Death, so it be but glorious? 'Tis a sunset;
> And mortals may be happy to resemble
> The Gods but in decay.
>
> (II, i, 33–36)

Byron's comparison of death to a sunset is scarcely extraordinary, but several features of the soliloquy relieve the metaphor of triteness, and, indeed, cause it to evolve spontaneously from the context. The entire passage is organized by an implicit generalization on the nature of man and god; and since the sun is a deity, the concluding metaphor is perfectly appropriate, for it crystallizes in an image the point of Beleses' remarks—the immeasurable difference between mortal and immortal existence. Furthermore, the priest's sober consciousness of this difference motivates his participation in the rebellion: although he despises Sardanapalus and loathes the demoralization of Assyria, he perceives in the conspiracy the opportunity to assert his own thwarted aspirations, a chance to insure his personal immortality, at least in the minds of future Assyrian generations. Beleses' apostrophe to the sun, therefore, serves three purposes: it establishes the sun as the primary deity of the drama; it provides motivation for the priest's alliance with the traitors; and, in a larger sense, it introduces the theme of man's aspirations toward godship as one of the major motifs of the tragedy.

To Arbaces' warning that his "devotions" waste time, Beleses counters with the reminder that "the very stars shine victory" for the conspirators. Thus Byron provides yet another subtle paradoxical preparation for Sardanapalus' spiritual triumph by associating light first with the planets and second with weapons of battle. Reiterating his assurance, Beleses points to the "earliest" and "brightest" of the orbs, "which so quivers / As it would quit its place in the blue ether. / . . . 'Tis thy natural ruler—thy birth planet." Arbaces too, then, aspires "beyond the fitting medium," for in the "quivering" of the star is the cunning hint that the planet would relocate itself elsewhere in the celestial scheme. But Arbaces has little respect for the priest's supernaturalism: "My star is in this scabbard," he insists; "when it shines, / It shall out-dazzle comets." Sardanapalus, we will see later, proves "brilliant" with his weapons, and hence aligns himself clearly with the light, the energy, and the divinity of the sun.

For the moment, however, concentration upon stars and starlight dominates the speculations of the characters. Particularly noteworthy is the king's subtle shift of emphasis, after the palace brawl, with respect to the existence of divine beings. Considerably less jaunty in bearing, less frivolous in thought, Sardanapalus now exchanges his earlier sophomoric atheism for studied agnosticism. Warned by Beleses that he should revere the stars, he admits that he loves them—for their similarity to Myrrah's eyes:

> but whether they may be
> Gods, as some say, or the abodes of Gods,
> As others hold, or simply lamps of night,
> Worlds—or the lights of Worlds—I know nor care not.
> There's something sweet in my uncertainty
> I would not change for your Chaldean lore;
> Besides, I know of these all clay can know
> Of aught above it, or below it—nothing.
> I see their brilliancy and feel their beauty—
> When they shine on my grave I shall know neither.
> (II, i, 259–268)

Beyond the association of hypothetical gods with stars and Sardana-

palus' cautious search among various alternatives for the true significance of the planets, the passage paradoxically discloses first the
king's pose of indifference with regard to theological concerns, and
second, his attempt to reconcile himself to the limitations of mortal
existence. Despite the claim that he neither knows nor cares, and the
belief that his knowledge encompasses "all that clay can know," the
fact is that Sardanapalus is no more reconciled to the physical and
intellectual limitations of human life than are Beleses and Arbaces.
Moreover, we may interpret the king's debauchery as an ineffectual
means of escape from awareness of life's nothingness—an attempt to
verify his identity in a world without meaning. Momentarily denied
the opportunity of escape through sensual excess by the outbreak of
violence, he is forced to confront squarely his own philosophical and
epistemological dilemma. Sardanapalus tries to escape once again by
affecting indifference, but the energy of his effort betrays a deeply
rooted fear that existence may after all be devoid of meaning. And
this fear, as much as anything else, launches the king on a campaign
to assert his own individuality, prove his own human worth, in the
imminent conflict.

As midnight, the hour of the banquet, approaches, "the air grows
thick and choking," and images of starlight are gradually replaced
not by the artificial light of the palace, but by the "forked flashes" of
a "commanding tempest." The interrelationship of light and divinity
continues, however, in the implicit belief among the revelers that
lightning is a visible manifestation, benevolent or malevolent—as the
occasion demands—of the gods' pleasure. Even Sardanapalus now
finds it proper to admit that "ever and anon some falling bolt"
proves the existence of heavenly beings. To Myrrah, the lightning
represents divine intervention in human affairs: the gods, she says,
"flash this storm between thee and thy foes, / To shield thee from
them." The introduction of lightning and storm references at this
point serves both a practical and a symbolic purpose: the seemingly
benevolent co-operation of Nature in royal affairs paradoxically foreshadows the malevolent inundation of the city's walls by the flooding
river in Act V; and the implied association of fire (lightning) with
divine creatures prepares for a similar association in Sardanapalus'
self-sacrifice. Hence, also, the inferential reference to the power and
omnipotence of the gods suggests the old theme of man's littleness

and impotence in comparison with divine beings. Thus lightning functions as a further stimulus to Sardanapalus' desire for individual immortality.

As the storm abates, the steady revealing light of the moon "breaks forth in her brightness" over the raging conflict. Amid the "moon's broad light," Sardanapalus, with "His silk tiara and his flowing hair," is a "mark too royal," but despite the danger, the king conducts himself in a manner thoroughly befitting his regal station. "This great hour," Salemenes remarks, "has proved / The brightest and most glorious of your life." The moon reigns over the action only temporarily, and its function within the framework of light imagery is less important (and less clear) than that of other luminary orbs. Perhaps it represents a kind of intermediary stage in Sardanapalus' psychological development: in its association with battle, moonlight illuminates the king's extreme absorption in military endeavor, revealing at once his removal from the sensual, artificial light of the pavilion, the decisive dedication of his abilities to masculine action, and, at least indirectly, his proximity to the sun.

The imagistic and thematic norms for the drama are supplied in Myrrah's beautiful apostrophe to the rising sun opening Act V—a speech which parallels Beleses' address to the setting sun in Act II. Organized around a series of antitheses (night-morning, beauty-ugliness, peace-war, heaven-earth, permanence-transience, appearance-reality, hope-despair, pain-pleasure, and divinity-mortality), her soliloquy unites in one massed declaration the various antipodal, abstract issues which the drama sets forth, and, in some cases, attempts to reconcile. All of them may be included under the single issue of the enormous disparity between the character and existence of man and god. The majesty of the dawn forces upon Myrrah the awareness of her own, and all humanity's, insignificance before the powerful, eternal sun-god[26]—the recognition of life's pettiness, chaos, and pain in comparison with divine nature. By placing the

---

26. Cf. V, i, 50–53, Myrrah to her attendant:

Myr.   never
Had earthly monarch half the power and glory
Which centres in a single ray of his.
Bal.   Surely he is a God!

apostrophe to the sun at this juncture of the action, Byron can figuratively summarize the philosophical and psychological issues, and
their accompanying associations with light imagery, which have thus
far preoccupied the poetry of the play. Moreover, by emphasizing at
such length the divine qualities of the sun, he explicitly prepares for
the numerous fire figures about to be introduced, and, by implication,
for Sardanapalus' climactic kinship with the sun.

The king's instructions for building the pyre around the throne are
minutely detailed and are delivered with an energetic decisiveness.
He is concerned lest the fire "speedily exhaust its own too subtle
flame," or lest the enemy should easily extinguish it. To Myrrah,
both because of her loyalty in adversity and her previous idolization
of the sun, Sardanapalus extends the privilege of lighting the torch
and firing the pile of fagots. But notice that to kindle the pile,
Myrrah chooses

> One of the torches which lie heaped beneath
> The ever-burning lamp that burns without,
> Before Baal's shrine . . . .
> > (V, i, 419–421)

Sardanapalus also is aware of the extent of his sacrifice, and, not
unjustly, of his messianic stature. "My fathers! whom I rejoin," he
cries,

> purified by death from some
> Of the gross stains of too material being,
> I would not leave your ancient first abode
> To the defilement of usurping bondmen;
> If I have not kept your inheritance
> As ye bequeathed it, this bright part of it [the palace],
>
> . . . .
> I bear with me
> To you in that absorbing element,
> Which most personifies the soul as leaving
> The least of matter unconsumed before
> Its fiery workings—and the light of this
> Most royal of funereal pyres shall be
> Not a mere pillar formed of cloud and flame,
> A beacon in the horizon for a day,

And then a mount of ashes—but a light
To lesson ages, rebel nations, and
Voluptuous princes.
(V, i, 424–442)

Still vaguely skeptical about the promise of an afterlife, Sardanapalus is nevertheless relieved to shed the bonds of "too material being," to purify the spirit of gross mortal stains in the purgative fire, to merge himself with the "absorbing element," having the assurance that he serves his ancestors and himself royally. He has in death secured earthly immortality, and his "divine" or messianic nature is imaged most skillfully in his association, initially with the fire from Baal's altar and, second, with the sun, the principal deity of the tragedy. The nobility of the king and the honor of Assyria are preserved and immortalized:

In this blazing palace,
And its enormous walls of reeking ruin,
We leave a nobler monument than Egypt
Hath piled in her brick mountains, o'er dead kings.
(V, i, 480–483)

The destruction of the palace and the king's concluding reference to monuments ties the pattern of light and fire imagery to another figurative motif established early in the drama. Sardanapalus, arguing with Salemenes against the evils of warfare and civilian slavery, takes pride in not having "sweated" his people "to build up pyramids / Or Babylonian walls." But Salemenes, ever conscious of the judgment of future generations, suggests that

these are trophies
More worthy of a people and their prince
Than songs, and lutes, and feasts, and concubines,
And lavished treasures, and contemned virtues.
(I, ii, 232–235)

Distilled in these two quotations are antithetical figures which represent opposing tendencies of the king's character, the one gradually replaced by the other as Sardanapalus moves away from sensualistic preoccupation toward emotional and intellectual equilibrium. On the one hand, images connoting lasciviousness and erotic luxury, of course, reflect the king's strong feminine impulses, while metallic, monumental, and statuesque figures are associated with his masculinity and the circumstances which activate it. Hence, in the opening scenes of the play, where the feminine impulse dominates, we hear much about the king's "sweating" in "palling pleasures" which dull his soul and sap his strength. His approach to the court is heralded not by trumpets but by the "lascivious tinklings" of lutes, lyres, timbrels, the "softening voices" of women, the "reeking odors" of "perfumed trains," the "bright gems of glittering girls." Sardanapalus seems more a slave to his own passions than a governor of his kingdom: Assyria is a "despotism of vice," where the evils of "sensual sloth . . . produce ten thousand tyrants." Living in "silken dalliance," the king and his courtiers leave "all things in the anarchy of sloth." Arbaces muses upon the ease with which he might take the throne, since only "drowsy guards and drunken courtiers" with "silken garments" protect the crown. Salemenes, anticipating the king's arrival in the palace, recalls how often Sardanapalus "Lolls crowned with roses." Sure enough, the stage directions instruct the king to enter "effiminately dressed, his Head crowned with Flowers;" and Myrrah later warns that "A king of feasts, and flowers, and wine, and revels, / And love, and mirth, was never king of glory." Still, the king will neither "forsake the goblet: / Nor crown me with a single rose the less." He longs for the day when he might retire with Myrrah to some secluded spot and "wear no crowns but those of flowers:" "we will sit / Crowned with fresh flowers like . . . sovereigns." Salemenes, fearing a reactivation of the king's feminine impulses and dubious of the security of the throne even after the expulsion of Beleses and Arbaces, believes that Sardanapalus is as free from danger "As he who treads on flowers is from the adder / Twined round their roots." And the king, finally repudiating his feminine tendencies, sees himself, in contrast to Salemenes, as "softer clay, impregnated with flowers." Byron has contrived these figures of self-indulgent luxuriance to include, and hence appeal to, the visual, tactual, auditory, olfactory, and gustatory senses. Certainly, as Sardanapalus gradually subdues his feminine inclinations, the images of softness decrease and finally disappear altogether; but in their abundance and variety, they suffuse two and one half acts of the tragedy with a feverish glow of sensualism.

But perhaps Byron's cleverest imagistic representation of Sardanapalus' growth from soft femininity to austere masculinity, and thence to an integration of the two predispositions, is the gradual symbolic transformation of the king's "distaff" first into a sword, and eventually into a sceptre. The poet prepares for the transformation early in Act I when Salemenes suggests to Sardanapalus, "They say thy sceptre's turned to that [a distaff] already."[27] Through Acts III and IV, of course, the king wields his weapons with uncompromising valor, but not until Act V does his masculine severity and reckless militarism resolve into steady humanitarianism, thus qualifying him to govern his domestic, political, *and* military affairs with calm, shrewd detachment. Only because the sceptre has degenerated into a distaff must Sardanapalus employ the sword: " 'Tis the sole sceptre left you now with safety," Salemenes warns. But at the conclusion the king can abandon the sword as he did the distaff, and, by resuming the sceptre and its noble responsibilities, can "make this sovereign dwelling what it was / A palace, not a prison nor a fortress."

My point here is that with Sardanapalus' change of character occurs a corresponding shift of imagistic emphasis from figures of softness and plasticity (or malleability) to figures of hardness and solidity. Conventional and usually unimpressive images of shields, swords, and armor of various sorts dominate the battle sections of the play; but more important are the increasingly numerous (after Act II) references to the palace as fortress, marble monuments to former kings and warriors, temples and altars of the gods—all of these rock figures culminating in Sardanapalus' nightmare, where the loathsome spectres, he recounts, "turned upon me," and stared,

---

27. Cf. I, ii, 414–418:

> Oh men! ye must be ruled with scythes, not sceptres,
> And mowed down like the grass, else all we reap
> Is rank abundance, and a rotten harvest
> Of discontents infecting the fair soil,
> Making a desert of fertility.

> Till I grew stone, as they seemed half to be,
> Yet breathing stone, for I felt life in them,
> And life in me: there was a horrid kind
> Of sympathy between us, as if they
> Had lost a part of death to come to me,
> And I the half of life to sit by them.
>
> (IV, i, 122–127)

The phantoms, he continues, were "like a row of statues," and so overcome by the spectacle is he that finally, "I sate, marble as they." The primary thematic association of these stone images is with ancestral heritage[28] and traditional value, but there is the strong suggestion in the nightmare sequence that Sardanapalus must temper with a degree of softness that portion of his character corresponding to the uncompromising hardness of Nimrod and Semiramis. The dream thus reveals to the king, as I have observed, the danger in intemperate masculinity, and hence makes a healthy compromise between his opposing impulses the most suitable solution.

The extremes to which the imbalance of Sardanapalus' character might lead him are imaged throughout the drama in figures of foulness, infection, and putrefaction which correspond in content, though not in intent, to a similar pattern already outlined in *Marino Faliero*. With the first news of the rebellion, for example, Sardanapalus responds bitterly: "the rank tongues" of his "vile herd" have proved themselves unworthy of aught save bondage. Still, he thinks well enough of himself for preserving the peace: he has not led his troops "To dry into the desert's dust," or "whiten with their bones the banks of Ganges" like the warring Semiramis. In a passage foreshadowing the nightmare scene and providing an early presentiment of the savagery in noble blood, Sardanapalus lashes out at Beleses and Arbaces:

28. Note especially Arbaces' remark:

> Methought he looked like Nimrod as he spoke,
> Even as the proud imperial statue stands
> Looking the monarch of the kings around it,
> And sways, while they but ornament, the temple.
>
> (II, i, 352–355)

> Were I the thing some think me,
> Your heads would now be dripping the last drops
> Of their attainted gore from the high gates
>   . . . into the dry dust.
> (II, i, 284–287)

But the impact of these figures seems mild indeed when compared to the appearance and accouterments of Nimrod and Semiramis. The "ghastly beldame" drips with "dusky gore;" she is the personification of loathsomeness:

>   —a grey-haired, withered, bloody-eyed,
> And bloody-handed, ghastly, ghostly thing,
>
> . . . .
>
> sneering with the passion
> Of vengeance, leering too with that of lust.
> (IV, i, 104–108)

Racing to plant her "noisome kisses" on the king's lips, she upsets the blood-filled goblets on the table, so that their "poisons flowed around us, till / Each formed a hideous river." The features of Nimrod are "a giant's," and his "long black locks curled down" like "serpent hair." The cumulative effect of these figures to some extent cripples their purpose, for their abundance and exaggeration suggest parody. Byron, however, was probably quite serious.[29] His intention in these figures of foulness and loathsomeness, I think, is to present as forcefully as possible the hazardous consequences of extreme passionate conduct, whether directed toward sensual pleasure or military conquest. Semiramis is guilty of intemperance in both areas—as is Sardanapalus briefly—but the nightmare, with all its hideous connotations, compels him to recognize the peril in excess, the nobility in moderation.

It is possible, moreover, to interpret Sardanapalus' escape from the dangers of excess as his emancipation from slavery to the vice of

---

29. Note Byron's awareness of the thin line between the tragic and comic elements of the play: " 'Sardanapalus,' " he wrote to Murray, "is . . . almost a comic character: but, for that matter, so is Richard the third" (*L & J*, V, 324; 22 July 1821).

sensual passion. Indeed, figures of captivity and freedom recur throughout the tragedy, and Myrrah the slave, we should recall, takes it upon herself to "free him from his vices." The king at the outset cannot consider his own "sins" or even the possibility of war with any degree of seriousness: at Salemenes' suggestion that the royal party remain within the palace, Sardanapalus quips, "What! am I then cooped? / Already captive?" But, submitting only to pacify Salemenes, he remarks: "If I must make a prison of our palace, / At least we'll wear our fetters jocundly." Again, however, Myrrah alone seems to perceive the real bondage in which all Assyrians live:

> I half forgot I was a slave:—where all
> Are slaves save One, and proud of servitude,
> So they are served in turn by something lower
> In the degree of bondage: we forget
> That shackles worn like ornaments no less
> Are chains.
> (III, i, 191–196)

Very slowly, principally through the influence of Myrrah, Sardanapalus recognizes not only his responsibility for the demoralization and sensual enslavement of his people, but also his individual unfitness for kingship. As the "very slave of Circumstance / And Impulse," he feels

> Misplaced upon the throne—misplaced in life.
> I know not what I could have been, but feel
> I am not what I should be . . . .
> (IV, i, 332–334)

By thus recognizing and admitting his faults, by bestirring himself in an effort to rectify them, and by liberating, in one climactic gesture, his "slaves" (both in the real and symbolic sense), Sardanapalus proves himself worthy of the sacrificial flames—frees himself from bondage to the senses.

Surpassing but thematically correlative with this slavery to passion, however, is man's inescapable bondage to mortality; and, as I have noted, the theme of the immense disparity between the nature of man and god organizes and integrates all other themes and image patterns in the tragedy. We have seen how Sardanapalus' gradual progress toward "divinity" is depicted in the harmonizing of his masculine and feminine impulses; in the actual and symbolic dawn of the sun; in the replacement of sensual, lascivious figures by metallic, statuesque configurations; and finally, in images of foulness and captivity—all of these having been explicitly or implicitly related along the way to some aspect of supernaturalism, godship, or immortality. The characters are steadily aware of their finitude, their petty triviality, their heavy burden of mortality in the face of infinity, omnipotence, divinity. And as though Byron already had his next play in mind, he allows Myrrah, in the most telling imagistic statement of his overruling theme, wishfully to speculate:

> If there be indeed
> A shore where Mind survives, 'twill be as Mind
> All unincorporate: or if there flits
> A shadow of this cumbrous clog of clay,
> Which stalks, methinks, between our souls and heaven,
> And fetters us to earth—at least the phantom,
> Whate'er it have to fear, will not fear Death.
> (IV, i, 56–62)

III

Byron of course had *Cain*[30] in mind long before he began work on *Sardanapalus*. The character of Cain and the account of the first fratricide had intrigued his imagination since his introduction in early childhood to Gessner's *Death of Abel*.[31] Additionally, if ever there was one historical or mythological personage who fully commanded Byron's spiritual and intellectual sympathy, that character was Cain. But despite the outrage of nineteenth-century moralists over the theological audacity of the play, and the parallel emphasis of many scholars on the drama's metaphysical cruxes and autobiographical revelations, *Cain* is substantially more than a theosophic tract recounting the poet's own implicit denial of religious orthodoxy. Byron himself, and

30. Significant remarks by Byron on the tragedy, and selections from contemporary reviews of *Cain* may be found in *L & J*, V, 368, 469–470; VI, 16, 23–24, 38–39, 48–49, 76–77, 140, and 155.
31. See Chew, pp. 118ff.

his more sensitive contemporaries, recognized the superiority of the play's poetry. To Murray, Byron wrote, "I think that it [*Cain*] contains some poetry, being in the style of '*Manfred*'."[32] "In my opinion," Shelley exclaimed to Gisborne, *Cain* "contains finer poetry than has appeared in England since the publication of *Paradise Regained*. *Cain* is apocalyptic—it is a revelation not before communicated to man."[33] Sir Walter Scott insisted that Byron had "matched Milton on his own ground";[34] the enraptured Thomas Moore declared that Aeschylus dwindled by comparison;[35] and even Goethe chimed, "Its beauty is such as we shall not see a second time in the world."[36] Such praise is amicable enough but sadly undiscriminating, for the drama is by no means as flawless as these acclaims would allow. My point is that the theological issues of *Cain* must not be extracted from the poetic and dramatic contexts in which they appear, since the philosophy of the drama is at once supported by and organically integrated with its poetry. The real effect of the tragedy depends rather more on the grandiloquent and functional poetry than on the sophomoric and bland philosophizing.

Besides, Byron articulated the philosophical theme of his tragedy more coherently than have many of his critics.

The object of the Demon is to *depress* him [Cain] still further in his own estimation than he was before, by showing him infinite things and his own abasement, till he falls into the frame of mind that leads to the Catastrophe, from mere *internal* irritation, *not* premeditation, or envy of *Abel* (which would have made him contemptible), but from the rage and fury against the inadequacy of his state to his conceptions, and which discharges itself rather against Life, and the Author of Life, than the mere living.[37]

---

32. *L & J*, V, 360 (10 September 1821). The parallels with *Manfred* are many and are cited by Coleridge, *PW*, V, 213–275.

33. Quoted in *PW*, V, 477, note 1. Shelley's admiration may have been in part due to the tangential similarity between *Cain* and *Prometheus Unbound*.

34. Letter to Murray, 4 December 1821; quoted in *PW*, V, 2–4. Scott may have been inclined also to uncritical exaggeration since the tragedy was dedicated to him.

35. *L & J*, 477, note 1.

36. Quoted in *PW*, V, 204.

37. Letter to Murray, 3 November 1821; *L & J*, V, 470.

Unable to achieve a synthesis between the thrusting mind and the thwarting flesh, Cain relieves his intellectual and emotional frustrations by slaying Abel, the representative of submission to divine authority and reconciliation to the limits of mortality. When the suspicion of his insignificance in the universe is visibly confirmed and intensified by the voyage through space, Cain retaliates with absolute action in an effort to establish his identity; and by the fratricide, he actualizes his contempt for a Creator who made him capable of defiance.

The five major figurative motifs to be considered here are familiar from my preceding discussions: blood-fire, organic nature, light-darkness, clay-dust, and the counterpart configuration. The matter of Genesis—the Fall, the expulsion from Paradise, the first fratricide, and the metaphorical use of light, fruit, fire, and blood—is of course perfectly suited to Byron's purposes in *Cain;* but as I hope to show, the poet elaborates and enriches these materials and strengthens the argument of the play by framing it in a refined and subtle imagistic construct.

When Eve, in an abrasive diatribe (III, i, 419–443) after her discovery of Abel's corpse, speaks of "fiery cherubim," she merely echoes Cain's frequent verbal assaults on the guardians of Eden's gates, whom, he says, "I see daily wave their fiery swords." Initially fearful of Lucifer, Cain reassures himself by recalling his courage before the "fire-armed angels," the "fiery-sworded cherubim" patrolling the boundaries of Paradise. As emissaries of God, these cherubim personify in aspect, character, and function what Cain considers the true nature of the deity—an empyreal god of vengeance and sadistic ill-humor whose favorite sport is the bullying of mankind. Cain's assumptions about the character of God are then verified when Abel's "burnt flesh-off'ring prospers better" than his own; indeed, "heaven licks up the flames when thick with blood." Abel's altar, he had remarked earlier, reeked with "its blood of lambs and kids"; and he scorned God's "high pleasure" in the "fumes of scorching flesh and smoking blood." "Thy God loves blood," he cries, and hastens to smash his brother's altar: "This bloody record / Shall not stand in the sun to shame creation." God, then, is a bloodthirsty, fire-consuming brute to Cain; and within the imagistic framework of the drama He is diametrically opposed to the sun and sunlight. Further-more, since Abel is divinely favored *because* his is a blood-and-fire-sacrifice, Cain's murderous act is a vicarious assault on God Himself. But ironically, Cain at the denouement is figuratively associated with that characteristic of God and Abel which he most abhorred: "My hand!" he exclaims, " 'tis all red and with . . . blood, / My broth-er's and my own." Baffled by the rationale of a Creator who creates but to encourage the destruction of those creations in sacrifices to Himself, Cain lashes out against this death-force as it is symbolized in the bloody oblations of his brother. But by unwittingly introducing death into the world, he paradoxically violates the most sacrosanct principle of his own character.

For Cain, again ironically and expressly opposed to divine nature, represents the life-force of the tragedy. His responsibility, together with Adah his wife, is to cultivate the land, to "cull" the "first fruits" from the earth:

> I am a tiller of the ground, and must
> Yield what it yieldeth to my toil—its fruit:
> Behold them in their various bloom and ripeness.
> (III, i, 217–219)

Galled by the necessity of sacrificing a portion of his produce, Cain is nevertheless proud of the earth's yield, and in his invocation to the deity he stresses the decency and naturalness of his offerings, in contrast to the distortion and perversion of Abel's: "the sweet and blooming fruits of earth . . . may seem / Good to thee, inasmuch as they have not / Suffered in limb or life." Cain is then grimly pleased when the renunciating whirlwind wrecks his altar and scatters his fruit; but, he conjectures, "Their seed will bear fresh fruit there ere the summer." Given Cain's agricultural profession, moreover, it is scarcely surprising that consciousness of the sacred trees and forbid-den fruits of Paradise weighs heavily upon him. His speculations, recriminations, self-justifications are thronged with references to the "bitter fruits," the "fruits of death" which are his exacting inherit-ance. He repeatedly emphasizes the absurd logic which caused God to "plant" the trees and then "prohibit" them. And in an ironic preparation for his later association with death, Cain prophesies,

> never
> Shall men love the remembrance of the man
> Who sowed the seed of evil and mankind
> In the same hour!
>
> (I, i, 441–444)

Furthermore, Cain's connection with reproductive process includes human procreation. Father of the infant Enoch, he metaphorically links his son with the cypress tree, and, remarking the "pure incarnation" of his cheeks, with "the rose leaves strewn beneath them." Multiplication of these examples is perhaps needless. The earthbound Cain consistently thinks and speaks in agricultural and reproductive terms. Thus the irony of his crime becomes all the more terrible and emphatic because murder is the supreme desecration of Cain's overruling passion. Abel's blood having sterilized the earth, the Angel of the Lord decrees to Cain, "when thou shalt till the ground, it shall not / Yield thee her strength"; and Cain, with dramatic and imagistic appropriateness, laments, "Oh, earth! / For all the fruits thou hast rendered to me, I / Give thee back this." Condemned to wander eternally in the wilderness and deprived of the single positive value he had cherished in life, Cain recognizes that in an impulsive act he has

> dried the fountain of a gentle race,
> . . . Which might have tempered this stern blood of mine,
> Uniting with our children Abel's offspring!
>
> (III, i, 557–559)

The suggestion in these lines that Abel might have functioned as a counterpart to his brother[38] recalls several references in the tragedy to the physical and spiritual affinity between Cain and Adah. I have already noted, particularly in connection with Manfred's relationship to Astarte and Sardanapalus' to Myrrah, Byron's unflagging interest in uniting his male heroes with a female counterpart who represents

---

38. The suggestion appears again in III, i, 535–537: Cain speaks of Abel:

> I, who sprung from the same womb with thee, drained
> The same breast, clasped thee often to my own,
> In fondness brotherly and boyish . . . .

some feature of that hero's personality or is a fulfillment of what he should become. But Byron, using the Biblical materials at his disposal, presents in *Cain* the most striking example of this counterpart figure in the person of Adah, Cain's wife and sister,[39] "Born on the same day, of the same womb."[40] Their marriage strengthens the sibling bond: they refer to and address each other as "brother" and "sister," almost never as husband, wife, or mate. The inseparability of their spirits is stressed again and again, perhaps most notably in Cain's response to Lucifer's question, "And dost thou love *thyself?*"

> Yes, but love more
> What makes my feelings more endurable,
> And is more than myself, because I love it.
> (II, ii, 320–322)

The insular and potentially happy domestic life of Cain and Adah is imaged in the physical similarity between them and their son: "Mother, and sire, and son, our features are / Reflected in each other." Clearly, there are similarities between Cain and Adah, but they are by no means spiritual twins: in their differences the importance of Adah as counterpart emerges. Where Cain is defiant, his wife is submissive;[41] where he is heretical, she is orthodox; where he is impulsive, she is patient; where he is bitterly frustrated, she remains placid and resigned; and when he is fatalistic, she counsels

---

39. We need not belabor any subliminal incest motif in *Cain;* suffice it to note that Byron knew he was treading thin ice. It is possible that he no longer cared, but he does have Lucifer observe that to love as Cain and Adah loved will one day be a sin in their children (I, i, 364–365).

40. Cf. Adah's similar remark:

> was not he [Cain] . . .
> Born of the same womb, in the same hour
> With me? did we not love each other?
> (I, i, 371–373)

41. But not always. Adah speaks of their

> expulsion from our home,
> And dread, and toil, and sweat, and heaviness,
> Remorse of that which was—and hope of that
> Which cometh not.
> (I, i, 358–361)

perseverance and faith. She exercises upon her brother a strong and potent influence; indeed, Adah alone can bend Cain's stubborn will to conform with her own or with God's. "Rather than see her weep," Cain admits to Lucifer, "I would . . . / Bear all—and worship aught." She "wrings" from him consent to offer a sacrifice in Act I, and after the disillusioning revelations of Cain's voyage, she performs the same function again in Act III. Even the "stars of heaven," which are to Cain the most beautiful of Nature's creations, "are nothing to my eyes and heart, / Like Adah's face." And after the judgment and condemnation by the Angel of the Lord, Adah, though herself guiltless, will with her husband "divide thy burden with thee." In one way, of course, Adah's performance in the drama does not really extend beyond that of a loyal, dutiful wife, and certainly the poetry in which her function is expressed does not rival Manfred's characterization of Astarte. But in the conception of Adah as both wife and twin sister of Cain, and in her representation as the spiritual and intellectual opposite of her husband, Byron epitomizes in a single image the closest approximation to total identification or unification possible between two human creatures: the physical (or sexual) desire for gratification, the emotional (or spiritual, or fraternal) impulse for correspondence with a kindred spirit, and the intellectual necessity for sympathetic communication (whether that communication be complementary or contradictory) between like minds, are joined and fulfilled in the relationship of Cain and Adah.

Byron, however, not content with figurative patterns which function apart from each other, complicates the procreative and countrapuntal motifs of the drama by correlating them with light images. Adah, returned from her morning labors, speaks of the lush fruits, "glowing as the light which ripens"; and Cain sacrifices his fruits "in the face / Of the broad sun which ripened them."[42] The imagistic association of sunlight with reproductivity is of course standard and familiar; even the opposition of light and blood is not

---

42. See also II, i, 100–104:

> Ye multiplying masses of increased
> And still-increasing lights!
> . . . where ye roll along, as I have seen
> The leaves along the limpid streams of Eden?

particularly noteworthy. But in view of our conclusions about the organic imagery in *Cain,* the implied dissociation of God here from active creativity strikes the first of several startling notes in Byron's use of light imagery in the play. These may be investigated in chronological order.

Adam, Eve, and Abel, as representatives of religious orthodoxy and submission to divine will, open the drama with unequivocal equations of God with light: their Creator was He "who out of darkness on the deep" made "Light on the waters with a word," who "didst name the day," who is invoked, "Jehovah, with returning light." Cain, however, introduces an opposing element: he recalls, with sour asperity, his wanderings "In twilight's hour to catch a glimpse of those / Gardens . . . Ere the night closes o'er the inhibited walls." Because He creates life merely to thwart, restrict, and eventually destroy it, God disqualifies Himself in Cain's thought from affiliation with light: rather, God and Death are regularly imaged in figures of darkness, or of shadowy, indistinct half-light, suggesting the circumscription, the inscrutability, and the blind ignorance which to Cain are the chief features of human existence, as well as of its Creator.

Tortured with such a conviction, Cain possesses but two sources of relief: one is his relationship with Adah; the other, paradoxically, is his sympathetic attachment to the planets: "I turned my weary eyes from off / Our native and forbidden Paradise," he mourns, "Up to the lights above us, in the azure." From darkness, from painful reminders of God's injustice and the inevitability of death, Cain turns to the stars, not because they are symbols of the Almighty, but because they represent apparent immortality, untainted beauty, exemption from mortal anguish and frustration. But while the planets may soothe Cain's agitated spirit, they also effect increased psychological irritation: in their infinite detachment from human affairs, in their seeming invulnerability to the corrosions of mortality, Cain perceives a symbolic manifestation of his Manichean aspiration toward disembodiment and immortality. Not the strictly divine, but the supernatural, suprapersonal aspect of the stars captures the imagination of Cain, at once placating and unsettling his spirit.

Yet Cain believes that his aspiration toward the planets is entirely consonant with his desire for infinite wisdom. Lucifer, drawing a similar comparison, suggests that the *spark* of knowledge in "young mortals" initiates their attraction to the stars. That Lucifer should be conversant with the distribution of knowledge among mortal and immortal creatures is in accordance with his status as a cherubim; but that he is of a lower order than the celestial angels is clear to Adah from the relative degree of his "brightness." God's angels, she confesses to him,

> are like to thee—
> And brighter, yet less beautiful and powerful
> In seeming: as the silent sunny noon,
> All light, they look upon us; but thou seem'st
> Like an ethereal night, where long white clouds
> Streak the deep purple, and unnumbered stars
> Spangle the wonderful mysterious vault
> With things that look as if they would be suns . . .
> Not dazzling, and yet drawing us to them,
> They fill my eyes with tears, and so dost thou.
>   (I, i, 507–517)

Several points in this passage are crucial in Byron's developing pattern of light imagery. The partial, and ominous, obfuscation of the nimbus around Lucifer and the comparison of his appearance to an "ethereal night" anticipate the literal and figurative darkness which steadily settles over the action as catastrophe threatens. In opposition to the "silent, sunny" noonlight of God's angels, Lucifer is explicitly linked to the inscrutable mystery and haunting beauty of the stars; and Adah's reference to the planets as "things that look as if they would be suns" ironically crystallizes in a single statement both the cause of Lucifer's "duskiness" and of Cain's imaginative attraction to the stars. But while the magnetism exerted on the characters by star- and Luciferian-light reduces Adah to a state of contemplative hypnosis, it stimulates Cain to an even more aggressive emotional and intellectual gravitation toward the heavens.

As a challenge to the capacity and endurance of Cain's imaginative faculties, then, Lucifer proposes the excursion through space and time. Cain is of course initially dazzled and intoxicated with the realization of his desires, the disclosure of galactic "myriads upon myriads" of stars. But as Cain recovers from original excitement over these phenomena, his rationality demands an explanation: the imaginative or aspiring faculty is gradually subdued and negated by the "clay" element:

> Ye multiplying masses of increased
> And still increasing lights! What are ye? what
> Is this blue wilderness . . .?
>
> (II, i, 100–102)

With the reactivation of the rational or mortal element amid the splendor of the imaginative and immortal realm, two things immediately occur: (1) beginning to sense his own dwarfishness, Cain recalls in the minutest detail certain incidents which he experienced in the "dim twilight" or the "night" of Earth and in near hysteria cries to Lucifer, "The earth! where is my earth? Let me look to it, / For I was made of it;" and (2) the brilliant clarity of celestial light slowly blurs into opacity. Lucifer feels neither responsibility nor inclination to reveal the mysteries of creation—if he comprehends them—but on perceiving the germ of the fulfillment of his purposes in Cain's dawning awareness of mortal insignificance, the diabolic angel hastily reinforces that awareness by escorting his pupil to the phantom realm. And Cain's first impression of this "phantasm of the world" is its pervasive deathlike pallor: " 'Tis a fearful light! / No sun, no moon, no lights innumerable." All, he notes, "Fades to a dreary twilight,"

> unlike the worlds
> We were approaching, which, begirt with light,
> Seemed full of life . . .
> And some emitting sparks, and some begirt
> With luminous belts, and floating moons, which took,
> Like them, the features of fair earth:—instead,
> All here seems dark and dreadful.
>
> (II, i, 181–189)

Evidenced through the length, the energy, and the emphases of Cain's references to the spheres he skirted in route to Hades are a deep dread of and a profound desire to avoid the darkness of death, as symbolized in the phantasmagoric shades of Hell. Increasingly more intimidated by the galaxies revealed to his vision, Cain recoils momentarily by remarking their similarity to Earth, which now, significantly, seems "fair" when compared to the spectral gloom around him. " 'Tis darkness," he groans, "So shadowy and so full of twilight"; and once more, appalled by these "interminable gloomy realms," he attempts to shake off the melancholy enveloping his spirit by recalling the splendors of other worlds. He wishes still to associate light with purity, immortality, beauty, life; but Lucifer has indisputably assured Cain that no part of the universe is free from the blemish of sin and the certainty of death.

Having suffered the abrogation of the value which he placed upon light, and having endured with little success the belittlement resulting from his exposure to universal immensities, Cain cannot undergo further psychological demoralization at the hands of Lucifer. He therefore meditates upon his one remaining positive value, Adah, whose beauty and importance to him now clearly transcend the value formerly given to light. The stars of heaven, the blaze of luminous orbs, the effulgent sun, the phosphorescence of the "noon of night"— all these, Cain affirms, "are nothing, to my eyes and heart, / Like Adah's face: I turn from earth and heaven / To gaze on it." By dissociating himself now from *earth* and *heaven*—that is, by negating the esteem with which he once regarded natural reproductivity and the light which made that process possible—Cain explicitly prepares for the physical enactment of his affinity with death. His attentiveness to Adah is therefore heavily ironic, for in the murder of Abel, Cain violates the principle of love and procreation (and the figurative connections of these with light) which Adah has now and again been made to represent.

Cain, then, returns to Earth, disenchanted, despairing, psychologically conditioned to impugn the force which endowed him with the desire but not the means for the fulfillment of his aspiring impulses. His mind dark with disillusionment, he notes that the cypress branches sheltering Enoch "shut out the sun like night." Speaking of the sun which he approached, he emphasizes its negative qualities, the "Worlds which he once shone on, and never more / Shall light, and worlds he never lit." And the light of Cain's eyes and countenance, suggesting not the life of sunbeams but the fiery glance of a vengeful god, "flashes with an unnatural light"; his "cheek is flushed with an unnatural hue." Finally, in lines reminiscent of the early fire images, the connections of those with a death-deity, and the light which suffused the realms of Hades, Eve speaks after the murder: "Ah! a livid light / Breaks through, as from a thundercloud." Cain is immediately and sincerely repentant; but he is now more fearful than ever of the dark: "Ere the sun declines," says Eve, "Let us depart, nor walk the wilderness / Under the cloud of night."

The tragedy of *Cain*, as Byron indicated, lies in the irreconcilable disparity between "his state" and "his conceptions." Juxtaposed against the representation of these "conceptions" in light images are configurations in which Cain's "state" is set forth in terms of dust and clay. The image is by now familiar, but Byron avoids the thinness and triteness which might result from such consistent exploitation of an imagistic motif in three ways: first, by thematically and ironically linking the clay figures to the metaphorical pattern of organic nature, and thence to the representation of Cain as a "tiller of the earth;" second, again ironically, by integrating the dust motif with the theme of living-death;[43] and third, by extending the application of clay images to inhabitants of unearthly realms. Possibly the clearest and most exquisite statement of the theme is given to Lucifer, who, after whetting Cain's intellectual appetite with hints of higher knowledge, inquires after his pupil's reaction. "I should be proud of thought," Cain responds, "Which knew such things." Lucifer continues:

> But if that high thought were
> Linked to a servile mass of matter—and,
> Knowing such things, aspiring to such things,
> And science still beyond them, were chained down
> To the most gross and petty paltry wants,
> All foul and fulsome—and the very best
> Of thine enjoyments a sweet degradation,
> A most enervating and filthy cheat
> To lure thee on to the renewal of
> Fresh souls and bodies, all foredoomed to be
> As frail and few so happy . . . .
>   (II, i, 50–60)

The statement amounts to a warning, but Cain, in his eagerness and naiveté, is oblivious to it. Only after repeated admonitions from Lucifer, joined with the revelations of spatial and temporal infini-

---

43. See particularly: I, i, 109–115, 171–176, 355–358; II, i, 50–60 and ii, 331–335.

tudes, does Cain fully understand the limits of mortality. "Thou art clay," Lucifer reminds him, "and can but comprehend / That which was clay." But Cain is insistent: whatever the demonic angel chooses to disclose, he has the capacity to apprehend. Lucifer despairs of patience:

> Thy human mind hath scarcely grasp to gather
> The little I have shown thee into calm
> And clear thought: and *thou* wouldst go on aspiring
> To the great double Mysteries! the *two Principles!*
> And gaze upon them on their secret thrones!
> Dust! limit thy ambition . . . .
>   (II, ii, 401–406)

Cain, however, as we have observed, cannot limit the thrusting impulses of his mind, and finally releases his intellectual frustration in the reckless and primarily emotional act of murder executed on God's representative. He can locate no reason for gratitude to the deity; for "being dust," and "grovelling in the dust," until he "return to dust," seems to Cain the sum of human experience. With light, life, fertility, knowledge, and immortality denied him, he can, perhaps justifiably, "look the Omnipotent tyrant in / His everlasting face, and tell him that / His evil is not good!"—can, in fact, defy a god who amuses himself by "flattering dust with glimpses of / Eden and Immortality," only to resolve it "back to dust again."

From the commencement of his career, Byron employed, in a variety of ways and with increasing success, what I have called a quartet of preferred imagistic motifs to figure forth the antipodal inclinations of human thought and conduct, and the difficulty, if not the impossibility, of achieving a reconciliation between them. The dialectical structure of his metaphors—largely responsible for their emotional and intellectual tension—remains much the same through the poems examined here; but Byron's systematic growth in artistic craftsmanship is obvious when one compares the cautious, exploratory use of imagery in the oriental tales with the configurative skill evidenced by the later works, where metaphorical patterns are structurally and thematically essential to total poetic communication.

Index

Abrams, Meyer H., 16*n*
Aeschylus, 140
Alastor (Shelley), 83
Alfieri, Vittorio, 98, 98*n*, 99
Alpinula, Julia, 71

Baal, 127, 133
Bacchus, 127
Blackstone, Bernard, 15*n*
Bloom, Harold, 3*n*, 5, 59, 59*n*, 73*n*, 81*n*
Bonaparte, Napoleon, 56, 63, 64–65, 67, 69, 107
Bostetter, Edward E., 55*n*, 81*n*, 82*n*
Burning Oracle, The (Knight), 3*n*, 16*n*, 81*n*, 107*n*
Byron, Augusta Ada, 56, 57
Byron, George Gordon, 6th Lord: reputation, 3–4; and *mobilité*, 5, 40*n;* on process of composition, 5–6, 16–17; mechanistic philosophy, 6–7, 12; three periods of career, 9–11; Calvinism, 27; skepticism, 39–41; influence of Shelley, 39–41; influence of Wordsworth, 39–41; Neo-Platonism, 41; on *Manfred,* 81; influenced by Vittorio Alfieri, 98; on *Marino Faliero,* 102; on *Sardanapalus,* 118*n*
—qualities of poetry: imagery (defined), 7–8; classicism, 9, 98; irony, 9; romanticism, 9, 11; satire, 9; characters, 15, 17, 45, 54*n*, 83–84; narrative, 15; dramatic technique, 98–100, 118*n;* and dramatic unities, 98–99, 101*n*, 118*n*, 126
—recurring images: clay and dust, 8, 10, 61, 82, 84, 124, 139, 148, 150, 151; darkness, 8, 10, 11, 23–24, 107, 126, 141, 146–148, 149–150; *Doppelgänger* (counterpart), 8, 10, 11, 19, 26, 32, 49, 60, 65–66, 70–71, 72–75, 77–79, 82–94, 114*n*, 121–125, 141, 143*n*, 143–145; fire, 8, 10, 19–20, 23, 26, 33, 59, 62, 65–66, 68, 74, 88, 123, 126–127, 132, 133, 141, 142; light, 8, 11, 22–24, 33, 35, 48–49, 50–52, 60, 103, 106, 126–132, 141, 145–151;

animals and insects, 9, 54, 75, 78, 110–112, 122–123; lightning, 9, 34*n*, 56–57, 77, 78, 86, 90, 130–131; moonlight, 9, 23, 90, 91, 106, 107, 109–110, 131; mountains, 9, 56, 60, 67, 70, 71, 73, 76, 76–79, 85, 88, 90–91; reptiles, 9, 87, 103, 110–112, 137; stars, 9, 26, 60, 76, 85, 90, 92, 110, 126, 127, 129, 130, 146, 147; storms and tempests, 9, 57, 58, 66, 67, 76–77, 82, 85, 91, 130–131; sunlight, 9, 10, 23–24, 26, 27, 33, 47, 67, 74, 82, 93, 107–109, 110, 126, 127–129, 131–133, 142, 145–146; birds, 10, 48–49, 51–52, 53, 56–57, 60–61, 69–70, 77–78, 82, 88; chains, 10, 47, 49, 82, 138; ice and cold, 10, 19–20, 23, 32, 35, 67; natural growth, 10, 11, 19, 20, 29, 34, 50, 57, 58, 64, 67, 69, 74–75, 78, 103, 111–112, 113–115, 124, 134, 141, 142–143, 145; stones, 10, 11, 19, 34, 47, 78, 103, 113, 114–115, 124, 135–136; dreams, 21–23, 30, 34, 125, 125*n;* dawn, 23–24, 106–107, 108–110, 117, 131–132, 139; blood, 31, 87, 103, 115–118, 125, 141, 142, 145–146; sea, 31, 60, 67, 73, 90, 117; disease and decay, 34, 57, 136–137, 139; columns, 47, 61, 70–71, 78; auditory images, 48, 50, 51, 89, 134; caves and dungeons, 49–50, 57–58, 90; castles, 57, 65, 67–68, 78; sky and clouds, 73, 88, 91; lakes, 75–76
—recurring themes: death and mutability, 8, 10, 18, 29–30, 88, 92, 93, 131, 138–139, 146, 150; duality of man's nature, 8–9, 11, 19, 25, 29–30, 32–34, 52, 55, 55*n*, 58–59, 77, 86–87, 88–91, 107, 121, 128, 131, 139, 143–144, 150; appearance and reality, 10, 16–17, 25, 33, 63, 106, 131; freedom and liberty, 10, 49–50, 52–53, 54, 138; love, 18, 29, 55–56, 69, 78–81, 92, 121*n*–122*n*, 126; guilt, 24–25, 29–30, 32, 81, 84, 93, 112; nature, 24, 29, 40–44, 55–56, 60, 67–68, 69–70, 72, 73,

153

BYRON AND THE DYNAMICS OF META-
PHOR is an attempt to reappraise the art of
Byron's poetry, specifically the technical craftsmanship of the poet's works written between 1812
and 1822.

The author's thesis is that Byron's artistry
underwent an actual dialectic process; that is,
the craftsmanship of his poetry grew as it nour-
ished itself on the contradictions inherent in human existence. Professor Elledge contends that
Byron was not the self-conscious autobiographer
that most earlier critics have called him; he was
simply unable to divorce his works from the conflicts in his nature. Forever oscillating between
the poles of dualism and monism, Byron incorporated this personal, yet universal, dichotomy
into his poetry and later plays.

From the start of his career, he employed a
quartet of preferred imagistic motifs (fire and
clay; light and darkness; organic growth and
mechanical stasis; and the counterpart, or *Doppelgänger*, metaphor) to express the antitheses of
human thought and conduct and the difficulty,
if not the impossibility, of achieving a reconciliation between them.

As Byron increased in poetic sophistication,
his use of images matured from the one-dimen-
sional representation in his early Oriental poems
to the richly organic imagery that was essential
to the structure and themes of his later works.
The author discusses three of Byron's early poems
(*The Corsair, Lara,* and *Parisina*), three of his
best-known works (*The Prisoner of Chillon,
Childe Harold's Pilgrimage,* Canto III, and *Manfred*), and three plays (*Marino Faliero, Sardanapalus,* and *Cain*) in this work designed primarily for Byron scholars and for specialists in
nineteenth-century English literature.